D0389536

WITHDRAWN
UTSA LIBRARIES

A REFERENCE GUIDE

TO

ENGLISH, AMERICAN, AND CANADIAN

LITERATURE

A REFERENCE GUIDE
TO
ENGLISH, AMERICAN, AND CANADIAN
LITERATURE

*An Annotated Checklist of Bibliographical
and Other Reference Materials*

INGLIS F. BELL

JENNIFER GALLUP

UNIVERSITY OF BRITISH COLUMBIA PRESS
Vancouver

A REFERENCE GUIDE TO ENGLISH, AMERICAN, AND
CANADIAN LITERATURE:
AN ANNOTATED CHECKLIST OF BIBLIOGRAPHICAL AND
OTHER REFERENCE MATERIALS

© 1971 by The University of British Columbia.
All rights reserved.

First printed 1971
Reprinted 1972

*International Standard Book Number
(clothbound edition) 7748-0002-X*

*International Standard Book Number
(paperback edition) 7748-0003-8*

LIBRARY
University of Texas
At San Antonio

Printed in Canada

TABLE OF CONTENTS

Section B: INDIVIDUAL AUTHORS

ABBREVIATIONS

AES	Abstracts of English Studies
BRD	Book Review Digest
CBEL	Cambridge Bibliography of English Literature
DAB	Dictionary of American Biography
DCB	Dictionary of Canadian Biography
DNB	Dictionary of National Biography
EGLI	Essay and General Literature Index
LHUS	Spiller, Literary History of the United States
MHRA	Modern Humanities Research Association. Annual Bibliography of English Language and Literature
OED	Oxford English Dictionary
OHEL	Oxford History of English Literature
PMLA	Modern Language Association Publications. Annual International Bibliography
YWES	Year's Work in English Studies

PREFACE

This guide has been designed to provide a practical introduction to research. Since there are already a number of books providing the essentials of scholarly research for graduate studies, this guide aims to meet the specific needs of the undergraduate specializing in English. The annotations attempt to instruct or remind him that the works listed have definite uses and limitations and that some should be preferred over others. The graduate student may find this guide useful as a preliminary checklist, but he will not find here any national bibliographies, author bibliographies listing primary sources only, *Dissertation Abstracts* and other sources for dissertations, union lists, or original sources such as the *Stationer's Register* and *Term Catalogues*.

The organization departs from the usual pattern to provide what we consider to be the simplest approach for the undergraduate. The book is divided into two sections, one dealing with general reference books and the other with bibliographies of major authors. Each is preceded by a note on its use, indicating the most relevant references and giving examples of the order in which the items should be considered.

In Section A periodical indexes are grouped with other bibliographies and surveys rather than listed separately. Notes and cross-references direct the student to other tools that he might wish to consult (or at least should be aware of) when researching a particular topic. The arrangement is basically alphabetical, with the standard work (if one exists) listed first. Serial bibliographies and annual surveys are added at the end of each section in a separate alphabetic sequence.

Section B lists the major authors alphabetically while the bibliographies of criticism under each are arranged chronologically. The aim has been to select the best available material, rather than to provide an all-inclusive listing. Bibliographies of limited scope contained within such series as the *Twayne Series* or *Writers and their Work* are omitted. We have selected writers who play a prominent part in undergraduate courses and who have published major works in Britain, the United States, or Canada—such writers as Nabokov and Katherine Mansfield therefore have been included. Comprehensive secondary bibliographies do not yet exist for some major authors—T. S. Eliot is a notable example. In such cases, we have listed one or two of the more extensive bibliographies within recent works of criticism on the author or provided a "see" reference to the specific pages of a more general source. The subject index refers the student to more general sources for many important authors who do not have adequate bibliographic coverage. Some checklists on single works of major authors are included. These usually treat the work most likely to be studied in survey courses—such as *The Bridge* or *The Scarlet Letter*. Occasionally a checklist has been prepared for an author's more minor work, such as Milton's *Samson Agonistes*, while his major work, *Paradise Lost*, lacks one.

This guide would not have been possible without the sympathetic assistance of Mrs. Juliette Stevens. We would also like to acknowledge our indebtedness to Dr. Jane Fredeman for many useful suggestions.

Section A:

GENERAL

HOW TO USE THIS SECTION

Most of the items listed within Section A are bibliographic works which will facilitate the student's search for background information and critical comment. Any search for secondary material should usually begin with the subject section of the card catalogue, and this guide serves as a supplementary aid to be used in conjunction with the catalogue. Many headnotes in Section A therefore first lead the student to appropriate headings in the catalogue. These headings are taken from the seventh edition of the Library of Congress list of subject headings, as most university and college libraries in the United States and Canada follow this system. For many general topics of wide scope the catalogue provides the best starting point, while for topics involving more current or less-known authors or themes, or for more specific subjects, the catalogue may yield very little or nothing. Most subdivisions of Section A contain lists of further references; they and the annotations to the individual items should be consulted before the actual compilation of a bibliography is undertaken.

The remainder of Section A contains general reference tools providing brief factual information necessary for the textual understanding of a literary work—for example, an earlier meaning of a word or pun, a brief explanation of an allusion to mythology, or a capsule biography of an author.

SAMPLE TOPIC I. "Major Themes of Norman Mailer's Short Stories in the Decade 1950-1960."

Certain topics require the location of texts of poems, plays, short stories or essays by minor or contemporary authors whose works have not been collected, which have been altered in form since first publication, or which an author has later chosen to exclude from his canon. To find these, the indexes listed in Indexes to Collections (III) are invaluable. For this topic, consult:

Indexes to Collections: Short Story (III:3)
The Short Story (I:4:d)
The Twentieth Century (I:3:f)
The General Section (I:2:a).

SAMPLE TOPIC II. "The Effect of Leacock's Academic Life on his Writing."

Many topics concern the relation of an author's life to his work.

If there is no secondary bibliography or if it does not list a biography, one may often be found in the references listed in the general, period, and genre bibliographies of this guide, if the student is prepared to conduct a rather extensive search. These will often also mention published texts of the author's correspondence. Brief sketches of the lives of authors may often be found in the reference works listed in the Biography section (IV:1-5). For this topic, consult:

Biography: Canadian (IV:4)
Canadian Literature (I:2:d).

SAMPLE TOPIC III. "The Condition of London Slums as Depicted in Charles Dickens' *Bleak House*."

Biographical, historical, philosophical, social and cultural topics usually require background information. The subject file of the card catalogue will list many literary histories, critical surveys, social and intellectual histories, but for a selected list of some of the more outstanding ones, consult sections VII and VIII: 5 of this guide. These surveys are valuable not only in themselves but for the reading lists they contain. For this topic, consult:

Social and Intellectual History: General (VIII:5:a) and Nineteenth Century (VIII:5:b:v)
Dickens (B42-44) and the appropriate items in I:2-4.

SAMPLE TOPIC IV. "Celtic Themes in Yeats."

For topics involving the influence of motifs, themes, and other literatures on English literature and on individual authors, the sections devoted to Comparative Literature (VIII:2) and to Myth, Folklore and Symbolism (VIII:3) may provide references otherwise difficult to find. For this topic, consult:

Comparative Literature (VIII:2) and Myth, Folklore, and Symbolism (VIII:3)
Yeats (B230-232) and the appropriate items in I:2-4
For more specialized reference works on auxiliary subjects, the student may wish to consult other guides listed in I:1.

SAMPLE TOPIC V. "The Critical Reception of Hemingway's *Farewell to Arms*."

Often the student wishes to assess the popular or scholarly opinion of a work at the time of its publication. Major reviews of well-known modern authors are often included in secondary bibliographies (Section B) or listed in the general, period, and genre bibliographies of this guide. For a wider sample and for authors established before 1900, it is necessary to use the works listed in Book Reviews (II). For this topic, consult:

Hemingway (B94-96) and the appropriate items in I:2-4
   A110-112, A115.

I
BIBLIOGRAPHIES, INDEXES, AND ANNUAL SURVEYS

I:1 GUIDES

A1 Altick, Richard D[aniel] and Andrew Wright. *Selective Bibliography for the Study of English and American Literature.* 4th ed. N.Y.: Macmillan, 1971.

> The shortest and easiest to use of the general guides. Includes an excellent preface on the use of scholarly tools and sections for the advanced students on such subjects as anonymous and pseudonymous literature, analytical bibliography, the book trade, dissertations, paleography, and public records. Few annotations.

A2 Bond, Donald F[rederic]. *A Reference Guide to English Studies.* 2nd ed. Chicago: University of Chicago Pr., 1971.

> More extensive than Altick and Wright (A1) containing additional sections on descriptive bibliography and typography, genealogy and a large number of auxiliary subjects. Items relating specifically to American literature, although not American history or biography, are collected in a single section. Brief annotations indicate format, contents, or limitations of major items.

A3 Gohdes, Clarence [Louis] [Frank]. *Bibliographical Guide to the Study of the Literature of the U.S.A.* 3rd ed. rev. and enl. Durham, N.C.: Duke University Pr., 1970.

> Well annotated guide to the necessary materials for research in American literature. Chapters 1-19 deal with general reference guides, methodology, general catalogues, and indexes of American items, American history and the history of ideas and themes important in American literature. Chapters 20-34 subdivide periods, genres, and specialized themes in American literature. Chapter 35 lists further items on comparative and general literature.

A4   Kennedy, Arthur G[arfield] and Donald B. Sands. *A Concise Bibliography for Students of English.* 4th ed. Stanford, Calif.: Stanford University Pr., 1960.

> Contrary to the title, the most comprehensive of the guides, but in need of revision. Clearly divided into subjects, with extensive sections on periodicals, the English language, folklore and popular literature, journalism, and general reference works. Brief annotations often clarify contents. Chapter 5 is devoted to major modern works of criticism and interpretation.

I:2 GENERAL

I:2:a GREAT BRITAIN, UNITED STATES, AND CANADA

Here are listed the general reference tools covering English-speaking authors of all periods. The student requiring a comprehensive bibliography on a specific author should first consult Section B. In addition to the general works cited here, students should also remember to consult the appropriate area (British, American, or Canadian), period, and genre sections of this guide.

A5   *Annual Bibliography of English Language and Literature,* 1920-. Cambridge: Modern Humanities Research Association, 1921- *(MHRA* or *ABEL)*

> Use together with *PMLA* (A15) for a comprehensive annual listing of books, articles, doctoral dissertations, and reviews of language and literature. Contains an index of authors and subjects treated, and is therefore easier to use than *PMLA.* Time lag of approximately 2 years, and is therefore not as up-to-date as *PMLA.*

A6   Besterman, Theodore. *A World Bibliography of Bibliographies.* 4th ed. Lausanne: Societas Bibliographica, 1965. 5 vols.

> Universal in subject matter. Arranged by subject with an author index. Separately published bibliographies only. For bibliographies in periodicals, see Bibliographic Index (A7) and Howard-Hill (A24).

A7   *Bibliographic Index.* N.Y.: Wilson, 1938-

Especially useful for separate bibliographies on individual authors in periodicals.

A8   *British Humanities Index.* London: Library Association, 1962-

Continues the *Subject Index to Periodicals, 1919-1961.* A general, selective index, covering all subjects in the humanities. Should be used with *MHRA* (A5) and *PMLA* (A15) as a supplementary source for articles from British periodicals. Useful for the student who is looking for reviews or articles on recent writers. Updated by quarterly issues.

A9   "A Checklist of Explication," 1944-

Published annually in the index volumes of *Explicator* since 1945. Lists analyses in books and periodicals of novels, poems, and short stories by British and American authors. Indicates exact subject of an article within square brackets, when this is not self-evident from the title.

A10   *Essay and General Literature Index,* 1900-. N.Y.: Wilson, 1934- (*EGLI*)

Useful for up-to-date criticism on individual authors contained in lecture series, collections of essays, conference discussions, and Festschriften. Although *PMLA* (A15) also indexes some Festschriften and other collections, this is a good supplementary source for such material.

A11   *Goldentree Bibliographies in Language and Literature.* Ed. O. B. Hardison, Jr. N.Y.: Appleton-Century-Crofts, 1966-

A series of selective bibliographies on all periods, genres, major authors, and special subjects such as linguistics and literary criticism. Convenient guides for the undergraduate. Excludes unpublished dissertations, book reviews, and short notes and explications. Individual volumes published to date have been itemized throughout this guide.

A12   Houghton, Walter E[dwards], ed. *The Wellesley Index to Victorian Periodicals, 1824-1900.* Toronto: University of Toronto Pr., 1966-

Should be used together with *Poole's* (A16). When completed, this multi-volume work will provide a subject, book review, and author index to Victorian periodicals. Contains a tabular view of the contents of each periodical, issue by issue, with the exception of poetry, and cites the evidence in support of attributions of authorship. While useful mainly for contemporary criticism on Victorian authors, the index covers all subjects contained within Victorian periodicals.

A13   *Index to Little Magazines.* Denver: Swallow, 1948-

Indexes, articles and reviews of creative work of recent writers contained in established little magazines. Serves as a supplement to *PMLA* (A15) and *MHRA* (A5).

A14   *Literature and Language Bibliographies from the American Year Book, 1910-1919.* Ann Arbor, Mich.: Pierian Pr., 1970. (*Cumulated Bibliography Series,* 1)

Cumulates the literature and language bibliographies of the *American Year Book* (*1910-1919*), which *PMLA* (A15) continued, beginning with 1921. Subject and author indexes supplement the cumulated volume. Since many important serial bibliographies of literature and language begin after 1919, this cumulated bibliography is a useful source for the period 1910-1919.

A15   "MLA International Bibliography of Books and Articles on the Modern Languages and Literatures," 1921-

Published annually in the June issue of *PMLA* 1922-1969. Since 1969 issued separately. 1922-1957, restricted to American contributions; since 1957 lists contributions in the modern West European languages on the language and literature of all countries. Considerable duplication with *MHRA* (A5) but both should be consulted if a comprehensive bibliography is desired. Unlike *MHRA*, it lacks a subject index and omits book reviews. Sections devoted to such auxiliary subjects as linguistics, comparative literature and the history of criticism are more extensive than those in *MHRA*. More up-to-date than *MHRA*. Periodical abbreviations in many indexes, and bibliographies follow *PMLA*, but note that *MHRA*'s abbreviations sometimes vary from *PMLA*'s.

A16   Poole, William Frederick. *Poole's Index to Periodical Literature, 1802-1881.* N.Y.: Peter Smith, 1938.

Catch-word subject index to 90 British periodicals. *The Wellesley Index* (A12) will eventually supersede Poole's to a great extent. Reviews are entered under subject except for novels, plays, and poetry, which are entered under author.

A17   *Social Sciences and Humanities Index.* N.Y.: Wilson, 1921-

> Vol. 1-2, entitled *Reader's Guide to Periodical Literature Supplement*; vol. 3-52, entitled *International Index.*
> More up-to-date than either *MHRA* (A5) or *PMLA* (A15) and cumulates more quickly than *AES* (A19). Useful for the student who is looking for reviews or articles on recent writers. Indexes many of the major American journals, including *Studies in Philology, Modern Philology, Modern Language Quarterly, Modern Fiction Studies, Modern Drama, PMLA and Victorian Studies.*

A18   Tucker, Martin, ed. *The Critical Temper: A Survey of Modern Criticism on English and American Literature from the Beginnings to the Twentieth Century.* N.Y.: Ungar, 1969. 3 vols. (*A Library of Literary Criticism*)

> Excludes literature of the twentieth century. In form, this work is parallel to *Moulton's Library of Literary Criticism* (A117) and supplements Moulton, providing excerpts from criticism written in the twentieth century. Sources of excerpts are given, with full bibliographic data.

The following items are useful to the student who wishes to review the current literature in his field, or to find a critical judgement in the absence of a book review:

A19   *Abstracts of English Studies.* Boulder: University of Colorado, 1958- (*AES*)

> Published 10 times a year, with annual cumulations and both monthly and annual indexes. Approximately 1,100 journals are screened for articles dealing with English, American and Canadian language and literature. Does retrospective indexing when a new journal is introduced.

A20   *The Year's Work in English Studies,* 1919/20-. London: Murray, 1921- (*YWES*)

> A survey evaluating briefly the outstanding books and articles of the year. Since 1958, contains a separate chapter on American literature.

I:2:b ENGLISH LITERATURE
(Great Britain and Ireland)

A21   *The Cambridge Bibliography of English Literature.* Ed. F[rederick] W[ilse] Bateson. Cambridge: Cambridge University Pr., 1940. 4 vols.

> Vol. 1: 600-1660; vol. 2: 1660-1800; vol. 3: 1800-1900; vol. 4: Index. *Supplement*: vol. 5, ed. G. Watson. Cambridge: Cambridge University Pr., 1957.
>
> The standard bibliography of British authors giving a comprehensive list of editions and a selective list of books and articles on authors established by 1900. Includes many minor authors difficult to find in other sources, and bibliographies on the political, social, and educational background, prose and poetic style, and literary relations with other countries.
>
> The supplement (vol. 5) extends references to 1955, but is still restricted to authors established by 1900. Running headlines in vol. 5 refer to the original page and volume number, enabling the reader to use the index for both the original volumes and the supplement.
>
> A revision of the entire work under new editorship is now in process. See A25.

A22   Bateson, F[rederick] W[ilse]. *A Guide to English Literature.* 2nd ed. Chicago: Aldine Pub. Co., 1968.

> A guide to definitive and standard editions, biographies, literary histories, and critical readings on British authors. Old English is omitted. For Old English the student should consult Fisher (A45). For medieval, romantic and Victorian authors, the student should prefer Fisher (A45), Houtchens (A68), Raysor (A69), Faverty (A74) and Stevenson (A76), as the bibliographic data is more complete.

A23   *The Concise Cambridge Bibliography of English Literature.* Ed. G[eorge] Watson. Cambridge: Cambridge University Pr., 1958.

> Abridges the *CBEL* (A21) deleting most minor authors, and abbreviating both primary and secondary bibliographies. Important for the inclusion of some 80 new writers, expanding the time limit to 1950.

A24   Howard-Hill, T[revor] H[oward]. *Bibliography of British Literary Bibliographies*. Oxford: Clarendon Pr., 1969-

> About one-half of the work is devoted to a listing of bibliographies (both primary and secondary) on individual authors of Great Britain and Ireland. Lists bibliographies appearing in journals as well as items separately published.

A25   *The New Cambridge Bibliography of English Literature*. Ed. George Watson. Cambridge: Cambridge University Pr., 1969-

> A revision of A21. Vol. 3, 1800-1900 published in 1969.

For a review of current research in English literature, consult:

A26   *Studies in English Literature, 1500-1900*. Houston, Texas: Rice University Pr., 1961- (*SEL*)

> Each quarterly issue has a section entitled "Recent Studies" giving an evaluation and summary of the outstanding studies of the year in a specific period. The first issue of every year is devoted to the English Renaissance; the second, to Elizabethan and Jacobean drama; the third, to the Restoration and the Eighteenth Century; and the fourth, to the Nineteenth Century.

I:2:c AMERICAN LITERATURE

A27   Spiller, Robert E., [and others], eds. *Literary History of the United States*. 3rd ed. rev. N.Y.: Macmillan, 1963. 2 vols. (*LHUS* or Spiller)

> Vol. 2 is the basic and most comprehensive bibliography of American literature, listing both primary and secondary sources. It is divided into 4 sections: I, Guide to Resources; II, Bibliographies: Literature and Culture; III, Bibliographies: Movements and Influences; IV, Bibliographies: Individual Authors. The detailed subdivisions and index are of considerable aid in locating material in this vast work.

A28   Blanck, Jacob, comp. *Bibliography of American Literature*. New Haven, Conn.: Yale University Pr., 1955-

> A descriptive bibliography of the primary works of some 300 American authors from the revolution to 1930. Authors who died after 1930 are excluded. Aims to in-

clude all first editions and a brief description of any book, pamphlet, etc. containing the first appearance of any prose or poetry of the authors included. Provides a short list of secondary references, but prefer Spiller (A27).

A29   Bryer, Jackson R., ed. *Fifteen Modern American Authors: A Survey of Research and Criticism.* Durham, N.C.: Duke University Pr., 1969.

Modelled on Stovall (A33) and continues Stovall, covering authors of the twentieth century. Each chapter surveys the bibliography, editions, manuscripts and letters, biography and criticism. Covers Sherwood Anderson, Cather, Hart Crane, Dreiser, Eliot, Faulkner, Fitzgerald, Frost, Hemingway, O'Neill, Pound, E. A. Robinson, Steinbeck, Stevens, and Wolfe.

A30   Davis, Richard Beale. *American Literature through Bryant, 1585 - 1830.* N.Y.: Appleton - Century - Crofts, 1969. (*Goldentree Bibliographies in Language and Literature*)

Contains both primary and secondary bibliographies on a large number of lesser figures.

A31   Leary, Lewis G[aston]. *Articles on American Literature, 1900-1950.* Durham, N.C.: Duke University Pr., 1954. *1950-1967.* Durham, N.C.: Duke University Pr., 1970.

A revision and extension of the checklists in *American Literature* (A35) containing earlier articles from 1900-1929 and some items not noted by *American Literature* after 1929.

A32   Rubin, Louis D[ecimus], ed. *A Bibliographical Guide to the Study of Southern Literature.* Baton Rouge: Louisiana State University Pr., 1969.

Contains 23 bibliographic essays on specific topics concerning Southern literature and provides selective secondary bibliographies for over 200 Southern writers, including many minor authors difficult to find in other sources. An appendix provides brief entries on 68 additional writers of the Colonial South.

A33   Stovall, Floyd, ed. *Eight American Authors: A Review of Research and Criticism.* N.Y.: Norton, 1963.

Each chapter surveys the bibliography, editions, manuscripts and letters, biography and criticism, on Poe, Emerson, Hawthorne, Thoreau, Melville, Whitman, Mark Twain and Henry James. The last chapter is a bibliographical supplement for the years 1955-1962, prepared by J. Chesley Mathews.

A34   Turner, Darwin T. *Afro-American Writers*. N.Y.: Appleton-Century-Crofts, 1970. (*Goldentree Bibliographies in Language and Literature*)

A35   "Articles on American Literature Appearing in Current Periodicals," June 1929-

> Annotated checklist published in *American Literature* in the issues of Nov. 1929, Jan. 1930, May 1930, and since Mar. 1931, in each issue. Excludes book reviews. A more extensive listing than *PMLA* (A15) or *MHRA* (A5), although both include items not found here. Relatively good coverage for articles in foreign language journals. The bibliographies for the period 1929-1950 and 1950-1967 have been collected and issued in 2 volumes by Lewis Leary (A31).

The following items are useful to the student who wishes to review the current literature in his field, or to find a critical judgement in the absence of a book review:

A36   *American Literature Abstracts*: *A Review of Current Scholarship in the Field of American Literature*. San Jose, Calif.: San Jose State College, 1967-

> Contains non-evaluative summaries, and appears semi-annually, in December and June. Abstracts are divided into 4 chronological periods: 1607-1800, 1800-1865, 1865-1910, 1910-1967, followed by a "Book Review Consensus."

A37   *American Literary Scholarship*: *An Annual*. 1963-. Ed. James L. Woodress. Durham, N.C.: Duke University Pr., 1965-

> A review surveying the year's work in American literature, including special chapters on Emerson, Thoreau, Hawthorne, Melville, Whitman, Mark Twain, Henry James, Faulkner, Hemingway, and Fitzgerald.

See also: Millet, *Contemporary American Authors: A Critical Survey and 219 Bio-Bibliographies* (A240).

Taylor, *The Story of American Letters* (A241), pp. 483-490.

I:2:d CANADIAN LITERATURE

A38   Rome, David, comp. *Jews in Canadian Literature: A Bibliography*. Rev. ed. Montreal: Canadian Jewish Congress and Jewish Public Library, 1964. 2 vols.

A compilation of biographical notes, bibliography, and excerpts of criticism on Jewish Canadian authors, including A. M. Klein, Saul Bellow, Irving Layton, Mordecai Richler, Leonard Cohen, and Adele Wiseman.

A39   Watters, Reginald Eyre. *A Check List of Canadian Literature and Background Materials, 1628-1950*. Toronto: University of Toronto Pr., 1959.

Part I contains comprehensive listings of English-Canadian fiction, poetry and drama separately published up to 1950. Primary sources only. Part II is a selective list of books bearing on Canadian literature and culture under such subdivisions as bibliography, biography, education, essays, local history, religion, and travel.

A40   ———— and Inglis Freeman Bell. *On Canadian Literature, 1806-1960*. Toronto: University of Toronto Pr., 1966.

A checklist of articles, books, and theses on English-Canadian literature, its authors and language, excluding book reviews.

A41   "Annual Bibliography of Commonwealth Literature," 1964-

Published annually in *Journal of Commonwealth Literature* since 1965. Section on Canada contains an annual survey of creative writing, followed by bibliographies of individual authors, a listing of fiction, non-fiction, studies of individual authors, general studies, and current journals.

A42   "Canadian Literature: A Checklist," 1959-

Published annually in *Canadian Literature* since 1960, listing articles and books on literary history and criticism, fiction, poetry, drama, theatre, and language. A more extensive listing than *PMLA* (A15) although *PMLA* does include articles not found here. For a scholarly discussion and evaluation of many items entered here, see "Letters in

Canada" (A44). An emended cumulation of the annual lists has been prepared by Inglis F[reeman] Bell and Susan W. Port, eds. *Canadian Literature: Littérature Canadienne, 1959-1963: A Checklist of Creative and Critical Writings. A Canadian Literature Supplement.* Publications Centre: University of British Columbia, 1966.

A43   *Canadian Periodical Index,* 1927-. T o r o n t o: Public Libraries Branch, Ontario Dept. of Education, 1928-1947; Ottawa: Canadian Library Association, 1948-

An author and subject index to over 80 Canadian periodicals, including *Canadian Literature, Canadian Forum, Dalhousie Review, Culture* and the *University of Toronto Quarterly.* Book reviews are listed under the subject heading "Book Reviews." Useful for recent criticism on a Canadian author.

For a current review of research, consult:

A44   "Letters in Canada," 1935-

Published in *University of Toronto Quarterly* annually in the July issue since 1936. A critical survey of the year's work in poetry, fiction, social studies, criticism, biography and belles lettres in English, French, and other languages. Excludes periodical articles. Useful for critical commentary on Canadian authors difficult to find elsewhere.

See also: Klinck, *Literary History of Canada* (A242), pp. 853-867.

Pacey, *Creative Writing in Canada* (A243), pp. 283-300.

I:3 PERIOD

For period studies in drama, poetry, novel, short story, and essay, consult the bibliographies in section I:4:a-e.

I:3:a OLD ENGLISH AND MIDDLE ENGLISH TO 1500

A45   Fisher, J[ohn] H., ed. *The Medieval Literature of Western Europe.* N.Y.: The Modern Language Association, 1966.

Guide to definitive editions and a survey of scholarship on such topics as *Beowulf, Gawain, The Pearl, Piers Plowman,* Chaucer, Gower, Malory, and medieval drama.

A46   Fry, Donald K. *Beowulf and the Fight at Finnsburh*: *A Bibliography*. Charlottesville: University Pr. of Virginia, 1969.

   A convenient compilation of books, articles, reviews, and dissertations. Listing is by author with subject classification indicated by a code system.

A47   Greenfield, Stanley B. "Chapter XVI: An Old English Bibliographical Guide," in *Guide to English Literature*; *from Beowulf through Chaucer and Medieval Drama*, by David M. Zesmer. N.Y.: Barnes and Noble, 1961.

   Carefully selected and annotated with indispensable items starred. Emphasis is on contemporary thought and controversy. Attempts in many cases to offer a critical evaluation of the items entered.

A48   ———. "Chapter XVII: A Middle English Bibliographical Guide," in *Guide to English Literature*; *from Beowulf through Chaucer and Medieval Drama*, by David M. Zesmer. N.Y.: Barnes and Noble, 1961.

A49   Matthews, William, comp. *Old and Middle English Literature*. N.Y.: Appleton-Century-Crofts, 1968. (*Goldentree Bibliographies*)

   Contains bibliography of general, historical, and cultural background, literary background, poetics and language, as well as texts, translations and commentary on *Beowulf*, Malory, the Pearl Poet, Chaucer, Gower, Lydgate, *Piers Plowman*, Skelton, Dunbar, the fifteenth century English poets, and religious prose and drama.

A50   Robinson, Fred C. *Old English Literature: A Select Bibliography*. Toronto: University of Toronto Pr., 1970. (*Toronto Medieval Bibliographies*)

   Annotated bibliography of standard editions, books, monographs and articles selecting the most useful recent works on each subject. Most of the publications listed are in English.

A51   Severs, J[onathan] Burke, ed. *A Manual of the Writings in Middle English, 1050-1500*. By Members of the Middle English Group of the Modern Language Association of

America. New Haven, Conn.: Connecticut Academy of Arts and Sciences, 1967-

> A rewriting and expansion of Wells (A52) covering also the literature of the fifteenth century and the criticism written from 1945 to the early sixties. Volume I, on the Romances, published in 1967.

A52   Wells, John Edwin. *A Manual of the Writings in Middle English, 1050-1400.* New Haven, Conn.: Yale University Pr., 1916. Supplements 1-9, 1919-1945.

> Standard handbook to all the extant writings in print composed in England. Indicates for each item its probable date, its manuscripts, the dialect in which it was composed, and its source or sources when known. Abstracts contents of longer productions. "Bibliographical notes" at the end of each volume list editions and some criticism written up to 1946. A revision is now in process. See Severs (A51).

A53   "A Bibliography of American Periodical Literature," 1933-

> Bibliography of medieval studies published in each issue of *Speculum* since 1934. Until 1959 covered Canadian as well as American studies and was known as "Bibliography of Periodical Literature."

A54   "A Bibliography of Critical Arthurian Literature," 1936-1962.

> Published annually in *Modern Language Quarterly* in the June issue from 1940-1963. Continues Parry, John J. and Margaret Schlauch. *A Bibliography of Critical Arthurian Literature for the Years 1930-1935.* N.Y.: Modern Language Association, 1936. 2 vols. Lists books, reviews, and articles on the literature of the Arthurian cycle from the romances of the middle ages to the present. Continued by *Bulletin bibliographique de la société internationale arthurienne* (A55).

A55   *Bulletin bibliographique de la société internationale arthurienne,* 1948-. Paris: Société Internationale Arthurienne, 1949-

> The only annual bibliography for the Arthurian cycle after 1963. Unlike the bibliography in *Modern Language Quarterly* (A54) restricted to medieval Arthuriana.

See also: Bennett, *Chaucer and the Fifteenth Century* (A213), pp. 240-318.

Chambers, *English Literature at the Close of the Middle Ages* (A214), pp. 206-231.

Renwick and Orton, *The Beginnings of English Literature to Skelton, 1509* (A217), pp. 116-486.

Other literary histories and critical surveys listed in section VII:1:a.

I:3:b   RENAISSANCE TO 1660

A56   Berry, Lloyd E[ason], comp. *A Bibliography of Studies in Metaphysical Poetry, 1939-1960.* Madison: University of Wisconsin Pr., 1964.

> A continuation of Spencer (A59).

A57   *Elizabethan Bibliographies Supplements.* Ed. Charles A. Pennel. London: Nether Pr., 1967-

> A series of checklists arranged chronologically with author indexes, attempting to list all relevant material, except anthology texts, all M.A. theses, and Ph.D. dissertations other than American and English. Certain numbers broaden the scope to authors (1400-1700) not included in the Tannenbaum series (A60). Bibliographies on the more outstanding figures of this period are individually itemized in Section B.

A58   Lievsay, John L[eon], comp. *The Sixteenth Century: Skelton through Hooker.* N.Y.: Appleton-Century-Crofts, 1968. (*Goldentree Bibliographies*)

> Contains general bibliography on background studies, anonymous literature and translations, as well as checklists on many minor figures, containing collected editions, selections, biography, and criticism. Excludes most Scottish writers, dramatic works, and non-dramatic works of writers who lived into the seventeenth century.

A59   Spencer, Theodore and Mark Van Doren. *Studies in Metaphysical Poetry: Two Essays and a Bibliography.* N.Y.: Columbia University Pr., 1939.

Lists books and articles written from 1912-1938 on metaphysical poetry and on 12 poets, including Carew, Cowley, Crashaw, Donne, H e r b e r t, Marvell, Traherne, and Vaughan. Continued by Berry (A56).

A60 Tannenbaum, Samuel A[aron]. *Elizabethan Bibliographies.* N.Y.: S. A. Tannenbaum, Nos. 1-41, 1937-1950.

Concise bibliographies of early critical articles and books. Supplements published by Nether Pr. under the general editorship of Charles Pennel extend coverage to the sixties. See A57.

A61 "Recent Literature of the Renaissance: A Bibliography," 1916-

Published in *Studies in Philology* in the April issue, 1917-1961, then in the May issue. Lists references to books, articles, and reviews on Renaissance background and authors, including Shakespeare, Milton, and Spenser.

For a review of current research, consult:

A62 "Abstracts of Recent Studies," 1942-

Published in each issue of *Seventeenth Century News* since 1943, containing summaries of articles on Milton, Donne, Herbert, and other seventeenth century figures.

See also: "The English Renaissance," *SEL* (A26).

Bush, *English Literature in the Earlier Seventeenth Century, 1600-1660* (A220), pp. 461-668.

Lewis, *English Literature in the Sixteenth Century Excluding Drama* (A221), pp. 594-685.

Pinto, *The English Renaissance, 1510-1688* (A222), pp. 133-394.

Other literary histories and critical surveys listed in Section VII:1:b.

I:3:c RESTORATION AND THE EIGHTEENTH CENTURY (1660-1800)

A63 Cordasco, Francesco. *Eighteenth Century Bibliographies: Handlists of Critical Studies Relating to Smollett, Richard-*

son, Sterne, Fielding, Dibdin, 18th Century Medicine, the 18th Century Novel, Godwin, Gibbon, Young, and Burke. To Which is Added John P. Anderson's Bibliography of Smollett. Metuchen, N.J.: Scarecrow Pr., 1970.

Reprints of *Eighteenth Century Bibliographical Pamphlets,* nos. 1-12, compiled between 1947-1950.

A64   Modern Language Association of America. *Proceedings of the Neo-Classicism Conference, 1967-1968.* Ed. Paul J. Korshin. N.Y.: AMS Pr., 1970.

Contains a bibliography on neoclassicism, covering the years 1920-1968.

A65   Tobin, James E[dward]. *Eighteenth Century Literature and its Cultural Background: A Bibliography.* N.Y.: Biblo and Tanner, 1939.

Includes bibliographies of thought, journalism, and history as well as primary and secondary bibliographies of 169 major and minor authors.

A66   "English Literature, 1660-1800: A Current Bibliography," 1925-

Published annually in the April issue of *Philological Quarterly,* 1926-1948, then in the July issue. Lists significant books, articles and reviews, including critical and biographical material on individual authors and on the social, philosophic, scientific, and religious background of the time. The bibliographies for the period 1926-1960 have been collected and issued in: Crane, Ronald S. [and others], comps. *English Literature 1660-1800: A Bibliography of Modern Studies: Volume I, 1926-1938.* Princeton, N.J.: Princeton University Pr., 1950; *Volume II, 1939-1950.* (1952) comp. by Ronald S. Crane [and others]; *Volume III, 1951-1956.* (1962) comp. by Arthur Friedman [and others]; *Volume IV, 1957-1960.* (1962) comp. by Charles B. Woods [and others]. Index covering vols. III and IV by Gwin J. Kolb and Curt A. Zimansky (1962).

See also: "Restoration and the Eighteenth Century," *SEL* (A26).

Dobrée, *English Literature in the Early Eighteenth Century, 1700-1740* (A223), pp. 586-696.

Dyson and Butt, *Augustans and Romantics* (A224), pp. 151-329.

Sutherland, *English Literature of the Late Eighteenth Century* (A227), pp. 442-578.

Other literary histories and critical surveys listed in section VII:1:c.

I:3:d ROMANTIC PERIOD

A67   Fogle, Richard Harter, comp. *Romantic Poets and Prose Writers.* N.Y.: Appleton-Century-Crofts, 1967. (*Goldentree Bibliographies*)

Contains general bibliography on background studies, as well as checklists of editions, biography, and criticism on major authors of the period, including Blake, Byron, Coleridge, Keats, Shelley, Wordsworth, De Quincy, Hazlitt, Hunt, Lamb, and Landor.

A68   Houtchens, Carolyn Washburn and Lawrence Husten Houtchens, eds. *The English Romantic Poets and Essayists: A Review of Research and Criticism.* Rev. ed. N.Y.: Modern Language Association of America, 1966.

Each chapter surveys the bibliography, editions, manuscripts and letters, biography and criticism, on Blake, Southey, Campbell, Moore, Landor, Lamb, Hazlitt, Scott, Hunt, De Quincy, and Carlyle.

A69   Raysor, Thomas M[iddleton], ed. *The English Romantic Poets: A Review of Research.* Rev. ed. N.Y.: Modern Language Association of America, 1956.

Each chapter surveys the bibliography, editions, manuscripts and letters, biography and criticism, on Wordsworth, Coleridge, Byron, Shelley, Keats, and the Romantic movement.

A70   "Current Bibliography," 1952-

Published in *Keats-Shelley Journal* annually since 1953 in the winter issue, listing books and articles on Keats, Shelley, Byron, and Hunt. A compilation has been prepared by Green, David Bonnell and Edwin Graves Wilson, eds. *Keats, Shelley, Byron, Hunt, and Their Circles: A*

Bibliography: July 1, 1950-June 30, 1962. Lincoln: University of Nebraska Pr., 1964.

A71 "The Romantic Movement: A Selective and Critical Bibliography," 1936-

> From 1937-1949, published in the March issue of *ELH*; from 1950-1961, in the April issue of *Philological Quarterly*, then the Oct. issue, 1962-1964; since 1965, published annually as a supplement to the September issue of *English Language Notes*. Includes books, articles, and reviews about English and continental writers of the Romantic period.

See also: "Nineteenth Century," *SEL* (A26).

> Dyson and Butt, *Augustans and Romantics* (A224), pp. 151-329.

> Jack, *English Literature, 1815-1832* (A232), pp. 458-631.

> Renwick, *English Literature, 1789-1815* (A234), pp. 254-289.

> Other literary histories and critical surveys listed in section VII:1:b.

I:3:e VICTORIAN PERIOD

A72 Buckley, Jerome H[amilton], comp. *Victorian Poets and Prose Writers.* N.Y.: Appleton-Century-Crofts, 1966. (*Goldentree Bibliographies*)

> Contains a general bibliography on the social and political background, intellectual and literary history and anthologies, as well as checklists on 31 poets and essayists including editions, biography, and criticism. Excludes writers of fiction.

A73 Ehrsam, Theodore G[eorge] [and others], comps. *Bibliographies of Twelve Victorian Authors.* N.Y.: Wilson, 1936.

> Includes bibliographical, biographical, and critical articles, pamphlets, essays, books, master's and doctor's theses on Arnold, E. B. Browning, Clough, Fitzgerald, Hardy,

Kipling, Morris, C. G. Rossetti, D. G. Rossetti, Stevenson, Swinburne, and Tennyson. The references are complete to July, 1934. Supplement by Joseph Fucilla in "Bibliographies of Twelve Victorian Authors: A Supplement," *Modern Philology*, XXXVII, No. 1 (1939), 89-96.

A74   Faverty, Frederic E[verett], ed. *The Victorian Poets: A Guide to Research*. 2nd ed. Cambridge, Mass.: Harvard University Pr., 1968.

Each chapter surveys the bibliography, editions, manuscripts and letters, biography and criticism, on Tennyson, the Brownings, E. Fitzgerald, Clough, Arnold, Swinburne, the Pre-Raphaelites, Hopkins, and later Victorian poets.

A75   Fredeman, William E[van]. *Pre-Raphaelitism: A Bibliocritical Study*. Cambridge, Mass.: Harvard University Pr., 1965.

A comprehensive, critical guide divided into four parts: sources for bibliography; individual figures; bibliography of the Pre-Raphaelite movement; Pre-Raphaelite illustrations. See also: Faverty, *The Victorian Poets* (A74), pp. 252-316.

A76   Stevenson, Lionel, ed. *Victorian Fiction: A Guide to Research*. Cambridge, Mass.: Harvard University Pr., 1964.

Each chapter surveys the bibliography, editions, manuscripts and letters, biography and criticism, on 16 novelists, including Dickens, Thackeray, Trollope, the Brontës, Eliot, Meredith, and Hardy. Excludes R. L. Stevenson, Samuel Butler and Henry James.

A77   "Victorian Bibliography," 1932-

From 1933-1956, published in the May issue of *Modern Philology*; from 1957-1958, in the fourth issue of *Victorian Studies*. Lists books, articles and reviews on Victorian times and literature. The bibliographies for the period 1932-1954 have been collected in Templeman, William D., ed. *Bibliographies of Studies in Victorian Literature, 1932-1949*. Urbana: University of Illinois Pr., 1945. *1945-1954* (1956) ed. Austin Wright; *1955-1964* (1967) ed. Robert C. Slack.

A78   "The Year's Work in Victorian Poetry," 1963-

Published in the summer issue of *Victorian Poetry* since 1964.

See also: "Nineteenth Century," *SEL* (A26).

Poole's Index (A16).

Wellesley Index (A12).

Jack, *English Literature, 1815-1832* (A232), pp. 458-631.

Other literary histories and critical surveys listed in Section VII:1:d.

I:3:f TWENTIETH CENTURY

A79 Gerber, Helmut E., ed. *The Annotated Secondary Bibliography Series on English Literature in Transition (1880-1920)*. Dekalb: Northern Illinois University Pr., 1970.

> The volume on Maugham is the first in the series. Subsequent volumes will include Joseph Conrad, Thomas Hardy, E. M. Forster, John Galsworthy, and George Gissing.

A80 Kherdian, David. *Six Poets of the San Francisco Renaissance: Portraits and Checklists.* Fresno, Calif.: Giglia Pr., 1965.

> Biographical notes and checklists of primary works (including translations, films, reviews, contributions, ephemera, etc.) on Lawrence Ferlinghetti, Gary Snyder, Philip Whalen, David Meltzer, Michael McClure, and Brother Antonius.

A81 "Current Bibliography," 1954-

> Published in each issue of *Twentieth Century Literature* since 1955. Abstracts articles.

A82 "Current Literature: I Prose, Poetry, and Drama," 1934-

> A survey of current creative writing published annually in *English Studies* since 1935.

See also: Stewart, *Eight Modern Writers* (A238), pp. 629-694.

> Other literary histories and critical surveys listed in Section VII:1:e.

I:4 GENRE

I:4:a DRAMA

I:4:a:i GENERAL

A83   Baker, Blanch M[erritt]. *Theatre and Allied Arts: A Guide to Books Dealing with the History, Criticism, and Technic of the Drama and Theatre and Related Arts and Crafts.* N.Y.: Wilson, 1952.

   An annotated bibliography of books published between 1885-1948. Subjects include history of the drama and theatre, biographies of actors and authors, and all aspects of stagecraft, including costume, dance, and music.

A84   Breed, Paul F[rancis] and Florence M. Sniderman, eds. *Dramatic Criticism Index: A Bibliography of Commentaries on Playwrights from Ibsen to the Avant-Garde.* Detroit: Gale Research Co., 1970.

A85   Coleman, Arthur and Gary R. Tyler. *Drama Criticism: A Checklist of Interpretation since 1940 of English and American Plays.* Denver: Swallow, 1966. Vol. 1.

   A list of criticism appearing in periodicals and books from 1940-1964, including Commonwealth and Irish drama. Author arrangement subdivided by title.

A86   *Cumulated Dramatic Index, 1909-1949.* Boston: G. K. Hall, 1965. 2 vols.

   An index to texts of plays whether published in book or magazine form and a checklist of critical, historical, and biographical articles on British and American theatre. Refers also to reviews of dramatic productions and screen plays. 1950-August 1953 published in *Bulletin of Bibliography*.

A87   Long, E. Hudson. *American Drama from its Beginnings to the Present.* N.Y.: Appleton - Century - Crofts, 1970. (*Goldentree Bibliographies*)

   Covers 26 major dramatists including Albee, Maxwell Anderson, T. S. Eliot, Arthur Miller, Clifford Odets, O'Neill, Elmer Rice, William Saroyan, Thornton Wilder, and Tennessee Williams. 27 minor dramatists are also included.

A88 Palmer, Helen H. and Anne Jane Dyson, comps. *American Drama Criticism.* Hamden, Conn.: Shoe String Pr., 1967. *Supplement I,* 1970.

Interpretations published between 1890-1968 in books, periodicals, and monographs, listed by playwright with the plays alphabetized under each author's name.

A89 ————, comps. *European Drama Criticism.* Hamden, Conn.: Shoe String Pr., 1968.

Lists books and articles written from 1900-1966 on British drama, excluding Shakespeare. Some foreign language material. Contains a section on miracle, morality, and mystery plays. Arranged by author with the plays alphabetized under each author's name.

A90 Salem, James M. *A Guide to Critical Reviews: Part I. American Drama from O'Neill to Albee.* N.Y.: Scarecrow Pr., 1966.

Refers to reviews of the theatrical productions of 52 playwrights, indexing American and Canadian periodicals, but excluding scholarly journals. Indexes the *New York Theatre Critics Reviews.*

A91 ————. *A Guide to Critical Reviews: Part III. British and Continental Drama from Ibsen to Pinter.* Metuchen, N. J.: Scarecrow Pr., 1968.

Limited to reviews of plays produced on the New York stage between 1909 and 1966. Indexes reviews from the same sources as A90.

A92 "Bibliographie," 1959-

Published in each issue of *Revue d'histoire du théâtre* since vol. 12, 1960. Extensive bibliography, including both biographical and critical articles on American, British, and European dramatists of all periods, as well as studies on all aspects of stagecraft.

I:4:a:ii PERIOD

A93 Henshaw, Millett. "A Survey of Studies in Medieval Drama:

1933-1950," *Progress of Medieval and Renaissance Studies in the United States and Canada. Bulletin*, No. 21 (1951), 7-35.

> An evaluative survey containing detailed bibliographical footnotes. Provides annotations for many items listed in Stratman (A94).

A94 Stratman, Carl J[oseph]. *Bibliography of Medieval Drama.* Berkeley and Los Angeles: University of California Pr., 1954.

> Bibliography of books, articles, reviews, and dissertations on all aspects of medieval drama. Provides also a guide to reference materials.

A95 Ribner, Irving, comp. *Tudor and Stuart Drama.* N.Y.: Appleton-Century-Crofts, 1966. (*Goldentree Bibliographies*)

> Contains basic reference works and bibliographical guides as well as critical and historical studies in general and on 22 dramatists, including Beaumont and Fletcher, Dekker, Ben Jonson, and Marlowe.

A96 Paine, Clarence S[ibley]. *The Comedy of Manners (1660-1700): A Reference Guide to the Comedy of the Restoration.* Boston: Faxon, 1941. (*Bulletin of Bibliography Pamphlets*, 36)

> Contains a general section on history and criticism, and individual entries for 7 dramatists, including Congreve, Farquhar, and Wycherley.

A97 "Restoration and 18th Century Theatre Research Bibliography," 1961-

> Selective annotated bibliography published annually in *Restoration and 18th Century Theatre Research* since 1962. A cumulation of the first annual bibliographies was published in: Stratman, Carl J., ed. *Restoration and 18th Century Theatre Research Bibliography, 1961-1968.* Troy, N.Y.: Whitston Pub. Co., 1969.

A98 Adelman, Irving and Rita Dworkin, comps. *Modern Drama: A Checklist of Critical Literature on 20th Century Plays.* Metuchen, N. J.: Scarecrow Pr., 1967.

> Indexes articles mainly in English on modern American,

British, and Continental dramatists, emphasizing critical material on the drama as literature.

A99   "Modern Drama: A Selective Bibliography of Works Published in English," 1959-

> Published in *Modern Drama* annually since 1960. Lists books and articles on drama and dramatists of all countries and periods.

See also: "Elizabethan and Jacobean Drama" and "Restoration Drama and the Eighteenth Century," *SEL* (A26).

Literary histories and critical surveys, section VII:4:b.

I:4:b NOVEL

A100   Bell, Inglis F[reeman] and Donald Baird. *The English Novel, 1578-1956: A Checklist of Twentieth Century Criticisms.* Denver: Swallow, 1959.

> A selection of major critical books and articles, listed under the individual works of each author.

A101   Gerstenberger, Donna [Lorine] and George Hendrick. *The American Novel, 1789-1959: A Checklist of Twentieth Century Criticism.* Denver: Swallow, 1961.

> Includes both general books and articles on novelists and the novel as a literary form, and critical interpretations of individual works.

A102   Holman, C[larence] C. Hugh, comp. *The American Novel through Henry James.* N.Y.: Appleton-Century-Crofts, 1966. (*Goldentree Bibliographies*)

> Contains general bibliography on American literary history, the novel as form, histories of the American novel, and special studies of the American novel, as well as checklists of texts, bibliography, biography and criticism on 42 novelists, including Mark Twain, Stephen Crane, Dreiser, Hawthorne, William Dean Howells, James, Melville, and Poe.

A103   Nevius, Blake, comp. *The American Novel: Sinclair Lewis to the Present.* N.Y.: Appleton-Century-Crofts, 1970. (*Goldentree Bibliographies*)

Contains general bibliography on American literary history, the novel as a form, histories of the American novel, and special studies of the American novel, as well as checklists on 48 novelists, containing texts, bibliography, biographical and critical books, biographical and critical essays.

A104   Stallman, Robert Wooster, comp. "A Selected Bibliography of Criticism of Modern Fiction," in *Critiques and Essays on Modern Fiction, 1920-1951*, ed. John W[atson] Aldridge. N.Y.: Ronald Pr., 1952, pp. 553-610.

Includes brief bibliographies on such topics as the problem of the artist in society, the artist and the creative process, the craft of fiction: technique and style, realism and naturalism, symbolism and myth, and checklists on individual authors.

A105   "Modern Fiction Newsletter," 1954-

Published in the summer and winter issues of *Modern Fiction Studies* since 1955. Contains critical reviews of current scholarship and a "roll call" restricted to works in English by and about writers of generally recognized stature.

A106   *Studies in the Novel.* Denton: North Texas State University, 1969-

Includes in the Winter issue an annual bibliography dealing with the history and criticism of the novel as genre, but excluding items on individual novels and novelists.

See also: Bennett, "An Annotated Bibliography of Selected Writings on English Prose Style" (A263).
———, "English Prose Style from Alfred to More: A Bibliography" (A264).

———, "Style in Twentieth Century British and American Fiction: A Bibliography" (A265).

Cordasco, "The 18th Century Novel," in *Eighteenth Century Bibliographies* (A63), pp. 145-165.

Modern Language Association of America. General Topics VI. *Literature and Society: A Selective Bibliography* (A279).

I:4:c: POETRY

A107   Kuntz, Joseph M[arshall]. *Poetry Explications: A Checklist
of Interpretation since 1925 of British and American
Poems Past and Present*. Rev. ed. Denver: Swallow,
1962.

>   Indexes interpretations in books and periodicals of poems
>   less than 500 lines.

I:4:d SHORT STORY

A108   Walker, Warren S., comp. *Twentieth Century Short Story
Explication: Interpretations, 1900-1966, of Short Fiction
Since 1800*. 2nd ed. Hamden, Conn.: Shoe String Pr.,
1967.

>   A convenient listing of books and articles on stories less
>   than 150 pages. Arranged by author with stories alpha-
>   betized under each author's name. Supersedes Thurston,
>   Jarvis [and others]. *Short Fiction Criticism*. Denver:
>   Swallow, 1960. Continued by *Studies in Short Fiction*
>   (A109).

A109   "Bibliography," 1962-

>   Published in each summer issue of *Studies in Short Fiction*
>   since 1963. Contains interpretive material on short fiction
>   in English, and continues Walker (A108).

I:4:e ESSAY

See: *EGLI* (A10) for critical material on essays listed by individual title.

II

BOOK REVIEWS

A110   *Book Review Digest*. Minneapolis: Wilson, 1905- (*BRD*)

>   An up-to-date digest and index to reviews in English and
>   American periodicals, arranged alphabetically by the

author of the book reviewed, with title and subject indexes. Largely restricted to journals that review books as soon as they are published, rather than the scholarly periodicals that publish reviews at a later date.

A111 *An Index to Book Reviews in the Humanities.* Detroit: Philip Thomson, March 1960-

Indexes reviews of books in English literature (both creative work and critical studies), history, philosophy, and fine arts. Both scholarly and popular magazines are included. Appears annually.

A112 *Book Review Index.* Detroit: Gale Research Co., Jan. 1965-

Covers a greater number and wider variety of periodicals than *BRD* (A110). Reviews listed under author of the book reviewed.

A113 Rogers, Amos Robert. *American Recognition of Canadian Authors Writing in English 1890-1960.* Ph.D. Thesis. Ann Arbor: University of Michigan, 1964. 2 vols.

Volume II, Appendix IX, pp. 670-813, lists book reviews on Canadian literature in American periodicals, 1890-1960.

See also: *American Literature Abstracts* (A36)

MHRA (A5)

Serial bibliographies listed in I:3, A54, A55, A61, A66, A70, A71, A77.

Index to Little Magazines (A13)

Poole's Index (A16)

Social Sciences and Humanities Index (A17)

Wellesley Index (A12)

For reviews of theatrical productions, consult:

Salem, *Guide to Critical Reviews*, pt. 1 (A90) and pt. 3 (A91).

Cumulated Dramatic Index, 1909-1949 (A86)

For reviews of Canadian books, consult:

"Letters in Canada" (A44);

Canadian Periodical Index (A43).

For early reviews, useful in determining how an author was received by his own contemporaries, there are several convenient compilations to consult:

A114   Allibone, S[amuel] Austin. *A Critical Dictionary of English Literature and British and American Authors Living and Deceased from the Earliest Accounts to the Latter Half of the Nineteenth Century.* Philadelphia: Lippincott, 1858. 3 vols.

>   Kirk, John Foster. *Supplement.* Philadelphia: Lippincott, 1891. 2 vols. Extends coverage to 1880. Contains excerpts from critical comments and reviews and cites sources. Bibliographic data is not as complete as *Moulton's Library of Literary Criticism* (A117). Supplement contains more authors of the latter half of the nineteenth century.

A115   Curley, Dorothy Nyren, Maurice Kramer, and Elaine Fialka Kramer, comps. and eds. *A Library of Literary Criticism: Modern American Literature.* 4th enl. ed. N.Y.: Ungar, 1969. 3 vols.

>   Contains excerpts from reviews and criticism on many minor and recent authors, difficult to find elsewhere. Cites exact sources with an index appended.

A116   Temple, Ruth Z. and Martin Tucker, eds. *A Library of Literary Criticism: Modern British Literature.* N.Y.: Ungar, 1966. 3 vols.

>   Covers more than 400 twentieth century authors, including excerpts from both books and articles and noting exact sources.

A117   Tucker, Martin, ed. *Moulton's Library of Literary Criticism of English and American Authors through the Beginning of the Twentieth Century.* Abr., rev. and with add. N.Y.: Ungar, 1966. 4 vols.

Based on Moulton's work, originally published in 1910. Excerpts from books, journals, letters, and manuscripts written mainly in the nineteenth century on literature from *Beowulf* to the present. Complete bibliographic data for the sources is given. The student should therefore prefer this work to Allibone (A114), although Allibone does contain some references not cited here. For criticism written in the twentieth century consult Tucker, *The Critical Temper* (A18).

For opinions on authors of the nineteenth century by their contemporaries, consult:

Poole's Index (A16)

Wellesley Index (A12)

III
INDEXES TO COLLECTIONS

If the student cannot locate the needed work in one of these indexes, he may also wish to consult the subject section of the card catalogue. General collections and anthologies are listed under the general heading: English Literature—Collections. There are also more specific headings for particular genres, such as: English Drama—Collections; English Poetry—Collections; English Prose Fiction—Collections (similarly for American and Canadian Literature). Short Stories, however, appear as: Short Stories, English—Collections; English Prose Fiction—Collections.

III:1 DRAMA

A118   Ottemiller, John H[enry]. *Index to Plays in Collections.* 4th ed., rev. and enl. N.Y.: Scarecrow Pr., 1964.

An author and title index to plays appearing in collections published between 1900 and 1962.

A119   Ireland, Norma Olin. *Index to Full Length Plays, 1944 to 1964*. Boston: Faxon, 1965.

> Alphabetical index combining subjects, titles, and authors of plays in collections and separately published.

A120   *Play Index*. N.Y.: Wilson, 1949-

> Three Series: 1949-1952, ed. Dorothy Herbert West and Dorothy Margaret Peake; 1953-1960, ed. Dorothy Margaret Peake and Estelle A. Fidell; 1961-1967, ed. Estelle A. Fidell. Lists plays that have been published separately, in the author's collected works, in collections, and in periodicals.

III:2 POETRY

A121   *Granger's Index to Poetry: Fifth Edition, Completely Revised and Enlarged, Indexing Anthologies Published through June 30, 1960*. Ed. William F. Bernhardt. N.Y.: Columbia University Pr., 1962.

> Indexes collections of poetry by author, title, subject, and first line. Supplement published in 1967 extends coverage to Dec. 1965.

III:3 SHORT STORY

A122   *Short Story Index*, 1949-. N.Y.: Wilson, 1953-

> Three supplements: 1950-1954, comps. Dorothy E. Cook and Estelle A. Fidell; 1955-1958, comps. Estelle A. Fidell and Esther V. Flory; 1959-1963, comp. Estelle A. Fidell.
>
> An index by author, title, and subject to stories appearing in collections. The 1953 volume compiled by Dorothy E. Cook and Isabel S. Munro supersedes Firkins, Ina Ten Eyck, comp. *Index to Plays, 1800-1926*. N.Y.: Wilson, 1927.

III:4 ESSAY

EGLI (A10) serves as an author index to essays appearing in collections.

IV

BIOGRAPHY

For an extensive biography of a well-known author, check first under the author's name in the subject section of the card catalogue. Other subject headings used for biography are: Authors, English; English Literature—Bio-bibliography. Similar headings are used for American and Canadian authors.

IV:1 UNIVERSAL

A123 *Biography Index: A Cumulative Index to Biographical Material in Books and Magazines.* 1946/July, 1949-. N.Y.: Wilson, 1949-

> Cumulates every 3 years; kept up-to-date by annual and quarterly issues. Excellent index to articles about authors of all periods.

A124 *Contemporary Authors.* Detroit: Gale Research Co., 1962-

> Contains living authors of current interest, including relatively new and unknown writers, with bibliographies of their works both published and in progress. 1962 appeared quarterly; since 1963 issued semi-annually. The latest annual volume always contains an index to all preceding volumes.

A125 *Current Biography.* N.Y.: Wilson, 1940-

> Contains articles about contemporary authors, primarily American, with a short list of references to books and articles. Issued 11 times a year. Annual cumulation includes index of all preceding years in the decade.

A126 Harte, Barbara and Carolyn Riley, eds. *200 Contemporary Authors: Bio-Bibliographies of Selected Leading Writers of Today with Critical and Personal Sidelights.* Detroit: Gale Research Co., 1969.

> An anthology of entries already published in *Contempo-*

rary Authors (A124). Many entries are revised and extended. Lists the author's contributions as well as his separately published works, and has a brief listing of biographical and critical sources. Especially useful for such authors as Ferlinghetti, Ginsberg, and Anais Nin, who are difficult to find elsewhere.

A127 Kunitz, Stanley J[asspon] and Howard Haycraft. *Twentieth Century Authors: A Biographical Dictionary of Modern Literature.* N.Y.: Wilson, 1942.

Covers all countries and includes bibliographies of works by and about each author. Latest printing revises death dates in notes.

IV:2 BRITISH

A128 *Dictionary of National Biography.* Eds. Leslie Stephen and Sidney Lee. London: Smith, Elder, 1885-1901. 22 vols. (*DNB*)

———. *1901-1911.* Ed. Sidney Lee, 1912.
———. *1912-1921.* Eds. H. W. C. David and J. R. H. Weaver. London: Oxford University Pr., 1927.
———. *1922-1930.* Ed. J. R. H. Weaver, 1937.
———. *1931-1940.* Ed. L. G. Wickham Legg, 1949.
———. *1941-1950.* Eds. L. G. Wickham Legg and E. T. Williams, 1959.
The standard work for British authors, containing scholarly articles with excellent bibliographies and including Commonwealth countries. Excludes living persons. The supplements extend coverage to 1950. For prominent British authors now living, see: *Contemporary Authors* (A124); *Current Biography* (A125); *Twentieth Century Authors* (A127); *Who's Who* (A132).

A129 Boase, Frederic. *Modern English Biography.* Truro, Eng.: Netherton and Worth, 1892-1921. 6 vols.

Contains "many thousand concise memoirs of persons who have died since the year 1850." Supplements *DNB* (A128).

A130 Kunitz, Stanley J[asspon] and Howard Haycraft, eds. *British Authors Before 1800: A Biographical Dictionary.* N.Y.: Wilson, 1952.

Biographical outlines with critical estimates, and short bibliographies of works by and about authors.

A131 ———, eds. *British Authors of the Nineteenth Century.* N.Y.: Wilson, 1936.

Biographical outlines with critical estimates, and short bibliographies of works by and about authors. Includes some authors of Commonwealth countries.

A132 *Who's Who.* London: Black, 1949-

Current volume useful for brief sketches on prominent British authors still living.

IV:3 AMERICAN

A133 *Dictionary of American Biography.* Eds. Allen Johnson and Dumas Malone. N.Y.: Scribner's, 1928-1936. 20 vols. (*DAB*)

———. *Volume XXI, Supplement One.* Ed. Harris E. Starr (1944). Additions to main *DAB*.
———. *Volume XXII, Supplement Two* (1958). Covers 1936-1940.
The American counterpart of the *DNB* (A128) containing scholarly articles with bibliographies appended and excluding living persons. Two supplements extend coverage to Dec. 31, 1940. For prominent living authors, see: *Contemporary Authors* (A124); *Current Biography* (A125); *Twentieth Century Authors* (A127); *Who's Who in America* (A137).

A134 Burke, W[illiam] J[eremiah] and Will D. Howe. *American Authors and Books: 1640 to the Present Day.* Aug. and rev. by Irving R. Weiss. N.Y.: Crown Publishers Inc., 1962.

An alphabetical dictionary containing information about authors, literary characters, novels, plays, poems, newspapers, and magazines. Contains more obscure and neglected authors than *The Oxford Companion to American Literature* (A150).

A135 Kunitz, Stanley J[asspon] and Howard Haycraft. *American Authors 1600-1900: A Biographical Dictionary of Ameri-*

can Literature. N.Y.: Wilson, 1938.

> Biographical outlines, critical estimates, and short bibliographies of works by and about authors.

A136 *The National Cyclopedia of American Biography*. Ed. James T. White. N.Y.: James T. White and Co., 1891-

> More comprehensive but less scholarly than the *DAB* (A133). The main series (51 vols.) covers people who are no longer living. Current volumes cover living people only, and appear about every six years. There is a general index to the whole series.

A137 *Who's Who in America*. Chicago: Marquis, 1899/1900-

> Current volume useful for brief sketches on prominent American authors still living.

See also: Kherdian, *Six Poets of the San Francisco Renaissance* (A80).

IV: 4 CANADIAN

A138 *Dictionary of Canadian Biography*. Toronto: University of Toronto Pr., 1966- (*DCB*)

> Aims to supply full, accurate, and concise biographies of noteworthy Canadians (exclusive of living persons), from the earliest historical period to the time of publication. Arranged chronologically with bibliographies appended. Two volumes now published, covering the years 1000 to 1740.

A139 *The Canadian Who's Who*. Toronto: Trans-Canada Pr., 1910-

> Current volume useful for brief sketches on prominent Canadian authors still living.

A140 Sylvestre, Guy, Brandon Conron and Carl F. Klinck, eds. *Canadian Writers: Écrivains Canadiens: A Bibliographical Dictionary*. New ed. rev. and enl. Toronto: Ryerson Pr., 1966.

> Sketches of prominent Canadian authors, with reference to critical articles about the writers.

See also: *Oxford Companion to Canadian Literature* (A151).

IV:5 THEATRE

A141   Rigdon, Walter, ed. *The Biographical Encyclopedia and Who's Who of the American Theatre.* N.Y.: Heineman, 1966.

   Biographies of American and European actors, directors, playwrights, designers, teachers, and others who have made notable contributions to the American theatre.

A142   *Who's Who in the Theatre.* Ed. Freda Gaye. 14th and Jubilee Ed. London: Pitman, 1967.

   Includes prominent living dramatists, critics, actors, directors, and producers, both English and American.

V
HANDBOOKS

V:1 GENERAL

A143   *Annals of English Literature, 1475-1950.* 2nd ed. Oxford: Clarendon Pr., 1961.

   Inclusive and reliable guide to the main literary output of each year. Records the publication of newspapers, periodicals, etc., and foreign events bearing on English literature. The index of authors gives a conspectus of each author's writings in chronological order.

A144   Benét, William Rose. *The Reader's Encyclopedia.* 2nd. ed. N.Y.: Crowell, 1965.

   An encyclopedia of literary terms, schools, trends, themes, characters, allusions, and authors.

A145   Fleischmann, Wolfgang Bernard, ed. *Encyclopedia of World Literature in the 20th Century.* N.Y.: Ungar, 1967.

Contains many extensive articles including an essay on modern English literature, vol. 1, pp. 333-351, with a useful bibliography appended; extensive biographical notes on leading modern authors with primary and secondary bibliographies; a chapter on literary criticism of England and the United States by René Welleck, vol. 2, pp. 311-325, with bibliography pp. 326-328.

A146 Freeman, William. *Dictionary of Fictional Characters.* London: Dent, 1963.

Includes the names of 20,000 fictional characters from English and American literature of all periods.

A147 Magill, Frank N[orthen], ed. *Cyclopedia of Literary Characters.* N.Y.: Harper and Row, 1963.

Contains an alphabetical character index of 11,949 names. Identifies obscure characters and gives a detailed analysis of major figures.

A148 ———, ed. *Masterpieces of World Literature in Digest Form.* N.Y.: Harper and Row, 1952-1960. 4 series.

Each entry contains a list of principal characters followed by a brief critique and a good plot summary. First 2 series limit coverage to the novel, drama, and epic poems; series 3 covers also lyric poetry and the essay.

A149 ———, ed. *Masterplots of American Literature: The Nineteenth Century.* N.Y.: Harper and Row, 1970. 5 vols.

Selections taken from *Masterpieces of World Literature* (A148).

A150 *The Oxford Companion to American Literature.* Ed. James D[avid] Hart. 4th ed. N.Y.: Oxford University Pr., 1965.

Concise information about American and Canadian authors, literary works, societies, terms, and allusions.

A151 *The Oxford Companion to Canadian History and Literature.* Ed. Norah Story. Toronto: Oxford University Pr., 1967.

Contains 450 literary entries, including biographical notes and survey articles on such topics as folklore, Indian legends and tales, literary magazines and fiction, short stories, drama, and poetry in English and French literature.

A152   *The Oxford Companion to English Literature.* Ed. Sir Paul Harvey. 4th ed. rev. Oxford: Clarendon Pr., 1967.

>Concise information about English authors, literary works, societies, terms, and allusions.

V:2 QUOTATIONS

A153   Bartlett, John. *Familiar Quotations.* 14th ed. rev. and enl. Boston: Little, Brown, 1968.

>Quotations, phrases, and proverbs, and their sources in ancient and modern literature, arranged by author with a concordance index. Best-known of the dictionaries of quotations.

A154   Brewer, Ebenezer Cobham. *Brewer's Dictionary of Phrase and Fable.* 9th ed. rev. N.Y.: Harper and Row, 1965.

>A collection of phrases and fables, explaining the origins of words and including information on the coinage of new phrases.

A155   Guinagh, Kevin, comp. *Dictionary of Foreign Phrases and Abbreviations.* N.Y.: Wilson, 1965.

>Includes proverbs, mottos, maxims, and a list of phrases arranged by languages. Excludes single words and items longer than a couplet.

A156   *The Oxford Dictionary of Quotations.* 2nd ed. London: Oxford University Pr., 1953.

>Arranged by author with a concordance index.

A157   Stevenson, Burton E[gbert]. *The Home Book of Quotations: Classical and Modern.* 10th ed. N.Y.: Dodd, Mead, 1967.

>Arranged by subject with a concordance index.

A158   Tilley, Morris Palmer. *A Dictionary of the Proverbs in England in the Sixteenth and Seventeenth Centuries.* Ann Arbor: University of Michigan Pr., 1950.

>A collection of the proverbs found in the literature and dictionaries of the period. Entered by subject with an index to significant words and a Shakespeare index, pp.

803-808, giving exact references. About 11,780 proverbs are listed.

See also: *OED* (A186).

Granger's Index to Poetry (A121).

V:3 LITERARY TERMS

A159   Thrall, William Flint and Addison Hibbard. *A Handbook to Literature*. Rev. and enlr. by C. Hugh Holman. N.Y.: Odyssey Pr., 1960.

> The most useful of the guides to literary terms used in current literary history and criticism. Good articles on point of view, satire, tragedy, naturalism and realism.

V:4 GENRE

V:4:a   DRAMA

A160   Altenbernd, Lynn and Leslie L. Lewis. *Handbook for the Study of Drama*. N.Y.: Macmillan, 1966.

> An elementary introduction to the elements of drama, dialogue and action, traditional types of plays and modern plays, with a brief reading list appended.

A161   Gassner, John and Edward Quinn, eds. *The Reader's Encyclopedia of World Drama*. N.Y.: Crowell, 1969.

> Sections on the drama of England, the United States, and Canada with bibliographies appended. Includes also biographical notes on playwrights, synopses, and historical background of individual plays.

A162   *The Oxford Companion to the Theatre*. Ed. Phyllis Hartnoll. 3rd ed. London: Oxford University Pr., 1967.

> Emphasis on popular rather than literary theatre; on actors rather than dramatists.

A163   Scholes, Robert E[dward] and Carl H. Klaus. *Elements of Drama*. N.Y.: Oxford University Pr., 1970.

A164   Shank, Theodore, J[unior], ed. *A Digest of 500 Plays: Plot Outlines and Production Notes.* N.Y.: Crowell-Collier Pr., 1963.

> Plays are arranged by country. Includes plot outlines and production notes.

A165   Sobel, Bernard. *The New Theatre Handbook and Digest of Plays.* N.Y.: Crown Publishers, 1959.

> Alphabetical dictionary of theatrical terms, biographical notices, articles on aspects of the theatre and drama, and digests of plays. A supplementary source; students should prefer *The Oxford Companion to the Theatre* (A162).

V:4:b   NOVEL

A166   Altenbernd, Lynn and Leslie L. Lewis. *Handbook for the Study of Fiction.* N.Y.: Macmillan, 1966.

> An elementary introduction to the elements of fiction with a brief reading list appended.

A167   Forster, E[dward] M[organ]. *Aspects of the Novel.* N.Y.: Harcourt, Brace, 1927.

> Not a handbook but an excellent source for definitions of such terms as plot, point of view, flat and round characters.

A168   Scholes, Robert E[dward]. *Elements of Fiction.* N.Y.: Oxford University Pr., 1968.

A169   ——— and Robert Kellogg. *The Nature of Narrative.* N.Y.: Oxford University Pr., 1966.

> Contains useful chapters on character, plot, and point of view in narrative, with bibliographical notes on each chapter.

V:4:c   POETRY

A170   Altenbernd, Lynn and Leslie L. Lewis. *Handbook for the Study of Poetry.* N.Y.: Macmillan, 1966.

> An elementary introduction to the language, form, and content of poetry, with a brief reading list appended.

A171   Hamer, Enid [Hope] [Porter]. *The Metres of English Poetry*. 4th ed. London: Methuen, 1951.

   Excellent introduction to versification.

A172   Preminger, Alex, ed. *Encyclopedia of Poetry and Poetics*. Princeton, N. J.: Princeton University Pr., 1965.

   Deals with prosody types, styles, ideas, movements, and the history and criticism of Western and non-Western poetry. Many articles survey the special literature and offer expertly selected, up-to-date bibliographies. Excludes entries on individual poets, poems, and allusions.

A173   Scholes, Robert E[dward]. *Elements of Poetry*. N.Y.: Oxford University Pr., 1969.

   Sections on metaphor, irony, music, metrics, and on how to approach a poem.

V:4:d   ESSAY

A174   Scholes, Robert E[dward] and Carl H. Klaus. *Elements of the Essay*. N.Y.: Oxford University Pr., 1970.

V:5 STYLE MANUALS AND USAGE DICTIONARIES

A175   *The MLA Style Sheet*. 2nd ed. N.Y.: Modern Language Association of America, 1970.

   The standard style sheet for students of English literature.

A176   Altick, Richard D[aniel]. *The Art of Literary Research*. N.Y.: Norton, 1963.

   Although the chapter entitled "Finding Materials" is now out-of-date, this work contains much information on the problems and methods of research, including sections on textual study, problems of authorship, the search for origins, and tracing reputation and influence.

A177   Barnet, Sylvan. *A Short Guide to Writing about Literature*. Boston: Little, Brown, 1968.

Provides a useful section on style and format; illustrative paragraphs on the role of setting in fiction, irony in drama, and figurative language in poetry; glossary of terms pertaining to rhythm and versification; sample essays on each genre.

A178 Bernstein, Theodore M[enline]. *The Careful Writer: A Modern Guide to English Usage.* N.Y.: Atheneum, 1965.

Covers word meanings, phrases, idioms, punctuation and other usage problems. Arranged alphabetically.

A179 Fowler, H[enry] W[atson]. *A Dictionary of Modern English Usage.* 2nd ed. rev. by Sir Ernest Gowers. Oxford: Clarendon Pr., 1965.

The standard guide to "correct usage." Fowler rejects much pedantic artificialism although he is inevitably an "instinctive grammatical moraliser." Gowers brings the work up-to-date without destroying any of the "Fowleresque" flavour. British point of view on pronunciation, spelling, and punctuation.

A180 Nicholson, Margaret. *A Dictionary of American-English Usage.* N.Y.: Oxford University Pr., 1957.

An adaptation of Fowler (A179) giving American variations.

A181 Sanders, Chauncey. *An Introduction to Research in English Literary History, with a Chapter on Research in Folklore by Stith Thompson.* N.Y.: Macmillan, 1952.

Contains chapters on problems in editing and biography and of authenticity and attribution, interpretation, technique, with suggestions on thesis writing giving specimen bibliographies.

A182 Seeber, Edward D[erbyshire]. *A Style Manual for Students Based on the MLA Style Sheet; for the Preparation of Term Papers, Essays, and Theses.* 2nd ed. rev. Bloomington: Indiana University Pr., 1966.

A183 Turabian, Kate L. *A Manual for Writers of Term Papers, Theses, and Dissertations.* 3rd ed. rev. Chicago: University of Chicago Pr., 1967.

A184   ———. *Student's Guide for Writing College Papers.* Chicago: University of Chicago Pr., 1963.

> In addition to providing information on footnote and bibliographic forms, acts as a guide to use of the library and how to plan and write a paper.

VI

DICTIONARIES

VI:1 GENERAL

A185   *American Heritage Dictionary of the English Language.* Ed. William Morris. Boston: American Heritage Publishing Co., 1969.

> Includes new words from science and technology as well as current social and cultural expressions. Excellent usage notes.

A186   *The Oxford English Dictionary.* Ed. James A[ugustus] H[enry] Murray. Oxford: Clarendon Pr., 1933. 13 vols. (*OED*)

> Indispensable reference work. Describes the history of every word, from the date of its introduction into the language, showing the development in meaning, spelling and pronunciation, with numerous illustrative quotations from the works of more than 5,000 authors of all periods. Supplemented by *Words and Phrases Index* (A189).

A187   *The Shorter Oxford English Dictionary on Historical Principles.* Rev. and ed. C. T. Onions. 3rd ed. Oxford: Clarendon Pr., 1962.

> An abridged form of the *OED* (A186), retaining a generous number of the illustrative quotations.

A188   *Webster's Third New International Dictionary of the English Language.* Ed. Philip Babcock Gove. Unabridged rev. ed. Springfield, Mass.: G. and C. Merriam, 1961.

The most useful dictionary for general purposes. Provides an excellent recording of widely-used language, both spoken and written, with illustrative quotations. Excludes many synonyms, antonyms, and Latin phrases found in the second edition.

A189 *Words and Phrases Index.* Comp. C. Edward Wall and Edward Przebienda. Ann Arbor, Mich.: Pierian Pr., 1969. 3 vols.

Lists antedatings, new words, new compounds, new meanings, and other published scholarship supplementing the *OED* (A186), *Dictionary of Americanisms* (A192), *Dictionary of American English* (A190), and other major dictionaries of the English language. Indexes articles on words and phrases in such journals as *Notes and Queries, American Notes and Queries,* and *American Speech.*

VI:2 REGIONAL AND DIALECT

A190 Craigie, Sir William A[lexander] and James R. Hulbert. *A Dictionary of American English on Historical Principles.* Chicago: University of Chicago Pr., 1938-1944. 4 vols.

Unlike Mathews (A192) includes "not only words or phrases which are clearly or apparently of American origin, or have greater currency here than elsewhere, but also every word denoting something which has a real connection with the development of the country and the history of its people." Contains illustrative quotations.

A191 *A Dictionary of Canadianisms on Historical Principles.* Ed. Walter [S.] Avis [and others]. Toronto: Gage, 1967.

"Canadianism" is interpreted as "a word, expression, or meaning which is native to Canada or which is distinctively characteristic of Canadian usage though not necessarily exclusive to Canada." Includes also Canadian pronunciations and alternative spellings.

A192 Mathews, Mitford M., ed. *A Dictionary of Americanisms.* Chicago: University of Chicago Pr., 1951. 2 vols.

Lists only words originating in America, and therefore includes fewer words than Craigie and Hulbert (A190).

A193   Wright, Joseph, ed. *The English Dialect Dictionary*. London: Henry Frowde, 1898. 6 vols.

> Attempts to include all English dialect words in use at any time since the beginning of the eighteenth century in England, Ireland, Scotland, and Wales. Gives etymology, pronunciation, and illustrative quotations from written sources.

VI:3 SLANG

A194   Partridge, Eric. *A Dictionary of Slang and Unconventional English*. 5th ed. London: Routledge and Kegan Paul, 1961. 2 vols.

> Includes colloquialisms, catch-phrases, nicknames, vulgarisms, and Americanisms. This edition includes the slang of World War II and many other new entries.

A195   Wentworth, Harold and Stuart Berg Flexner. *Dictionary of American Slang*. N.Y.: Crowell, 1967.

> Standard work covering all periods with emphasis on modern slang, and including a selective bibliography, pp. 655-669. Contains supplement by Flexner, including more than 1000 new slang terms.

VI:4 ETYMOLOGY

A196   *The Oxford Dictionary of English Etymology*. Ed. C. T. Onions. Oxford: Clarendon Pr., 1966.

> Contains some dates earlier than those recorded in *OED* (A186). Considers the development of spelling, pronunciation, and meaning as well as "origin and formation."

A197   Skeat, Rev. Walter W[illiam]. *An Etymological Dictionary of the English Language*. New ed. rev. and enl. Oxford: Clarendon Pr., 1909.

> Standard work, but not as reliable as *OED* (A186).

VI:5 SYNONYMS

A198   Roget, Peter Mark. *The Original Roget's Thesaurus of English Words and Phrases.* New ed. completely rev. and modernized by Robert A. Dutch. N.Y.: St. Martin's Pr., 1962.

> A collection of words and idiomatic expressions arranged according to the ideas they express, to aid one in locating apt and expressive words.

A199   *Webster's New Dictionary of Synonyms: A Dictionary of Discriminated Synonyms with Antonyms and Analogous and Contrasted Words.* Springfield, Mass.: G. and C. Merriam, 1968.

> A comprehensive dictionary of synonyms containing illustrative q u o t a t i o n s from classical and contemporary writers, and also indicating contexts in which words are not synonymous.

See also: *Webster's Third New International Dictionary of the English Language* (A188).

VI:6 SPECIAL PERIODS

A200   Bosworth, Joseph. *An Anglo-Saxon Dictionary.* Ed. and enl. by T. Northcote Toller. Oxford: Clarendon Pr., 1898.

> Toller, T. Northcote. ———, *Supplement*, 1921.
> Most comprehensive of the Old English dictionaries.

A201   Hall, John R[ichmond] Clark. *A Concise Anglo-Saxon Dictionary.* 4th ed. With a supplement by Herbert D. Meritt. Cambridge: Cambridge University Pr., 1960.

> Most convenient for the beginning student.

A202   Kurath, Hans and Sherman M. Kuhn, eds. *Middle English Dictionary.* Ann Arbor: University of Michigan Pr., 1952-

> Still in progress. Up to "J" in 1970. The dictionary intends to indicate the dialectal variants as well as the etymology and morphology of each word.

A203   Stratmann, Francis Henry. *A Middle-English Dictionary, Containing Words Used by English Writers from the Twelfth to the Fifteenth Century.* New ed. re-arr., rev. and enl. by Henry Bradley. London: Oxford University Pr., 1891.

> The most comprehensive Middle English dictionary in completed form. Gives quotations and citations from works of individual authors.

A204   Onions, C[harles] T[albot]. *A Shakespeare Glossary.* 2nd ed., rev. Oxford: Clarendon Pr., 1941.

> Gives definitions of words, with explanations and illustrative quotations. A corrected reprint was issued in 1946.

A205   Partridge, Eric. *Shakespeare's Bawdy: A Literary and Psychological Essay and a Comprehensive Glossary.* Rev. and enl. London: Routledge and Kegan Paul, 1968.

See also: *OED* (A186).

VII

LITERARY HISTORIES

AND

CRITICAL SURVEYS

This is a highly selective listing of literary histories and critical surveys. Many more can be found in the card catalogue under such headings as: English Literature—History and Criticism; American Literature—History and Criticism.

Period surveys may also be found under such headings as English Literature—18th Century—History and Criticism; American Literature—19th Century—History and Criticism. Surveys of the Anglo-Saxon period are listed under Anglo-Saxon Literature. Genre surveys are listed under such headings as English Fiction—History and Criticism; American Poetry—History and Criticism. Short Stories, however, appear under such headings as: Short Stories, American—History and Criticism.

This list should also be supplemented by the section on Social and Intellectual History, VIII:5.

VII:1 ENGLISH LITERATURE

VII:1:a GENERAL

A206 *The Oxford History of English Literature.* Ed. F. P. Wilson and Bonamy Dobrée. Oxford: Clarendon Pr., 1945- (*OHEL*)

> The most comprehensive of the surveys issued in a series although quality and comprehensiveness vary. Each volume contains an extensive annotated bibliography. Individual volumes are itemized separately in Section VII:1:b.

A207 Baugh, Albert Croll, ed. *A Literary History of England.* 2nd ed. N.Y.: Appleton-Century-Crofts, 1967.

> The standard one-volume history of the literature of England; revised edition contains a bibliographical supplement. Also published in 4 parts, individually itemized in section VII:1:b.

A208 *The Cambridge History of English Literature.* Ed. A. W. Ward and A. R. Waller. N.Y. and London: Putnam's, 1907-1933. 15 vols.

> Still an important general history of English literature. *OHEL* (A206) often offers a fuller, more scholarly treatment of authors. The bibliographies are out-of-date: consult instead, *CBEL* (A21).

A209 Dobrée, Bonamy, ed. *Introductions to English Literature.* London: Cresset Pr., 1939-1958. 5 vols.

> Each volume consists of a general survey of the period, bibliographies of the works of individual authors, and brief lists of biographical and critical material.

Individual volumes are separately itemized in section
VII:1:b.

A210   Ford, Boris. *The Pelican Guide to English Literature.*
Harmondsworth, Eng.: Penguin Books, 1957-1961. 7
vols.

    A general survey with studies of selected authors and
special aspects of the period. Includes chapters on the
social context of the literature and bio-bibliographies.

A211   Legouis, Emile H[yacinthe] and Louis F. Cazamian. *A
History of English Literature.* Rev. ed. London: Dent,
1960.

    Standard history, especially useful for the Pre-Romantic
and Romantic periods, with bibliographies by Donald
Davie and Pierre Legouis.

A212   Sampson, George. *The Concise Cambridge History of
English Literature.* 3rd ed. rev. London: Cambridge
University Pr., 1970.

    Contains additional chapters on the literature of the
United States and the mid-twentieth century literature of
the English-speaking world by R. C. Churchill.

See also: *MHRA* (A5) for a section entitled: "Literature, General:
Literary History."

VII:1:b PERIOD

VII:1:b:i: OLD AND MIDDLE ENGLISH TO 1500

A213   Bennett, H[enry] S[tanley]. *Chaucer and the Fifteenth
Century.* Oxford: Clarendon Pr., 1947. (*OHEL*, vol. 2,
pt. 1)

    Contains general chapters on religion, Chaucer and his
public, fifteenth century verse and prose. Selected bibliography, pp. 240-318, including a section on anonymous
writings.

A214   Chambers, E[dmund] K[erchever]. *English Literature at the
Close of the Middle Ages.* Oxford: Clarendon Pr., 1945.
(*OHEL*, vol. 2, pt. 2)

Covers medieval drama, the carol and the lyric, narrative poetry, the ballad, and Malory, with a selective bibliography, pp. 206-231.

A215   Loomis, Roger Sherman, ed. *Arthurian Literature in the Middle Ages: A Collaborative History.* Oxford: Clarendon Pr., 1959.

Separate chapters on the Welsh versions, Geoffrey of Monmouth, Layamon's *Brut*, the Breton Lais, the origin and growth of the Tristan legend, Gottfried von Strassburg, Chrétien de Troyes, the origin of the grail legend, the troubadours, *Gawain and the Green Knight*, and Sir Thomas Malory. Detailed bibliographical footnotes.

A216   Malone, Kemp and Albert C[roll] Baugh. *The Middle Ages (To 1500).* 2nd ed. N.Y.: Appleton-Century-Crofts, 1967. (Baugh, *A Literary History of England*, vol. 1)

Chapters on Caedmon and his school, Cynewulf and his school, the Arthurian legend to Layamon, *Piers Plowman* and other alliterative poems, Chaucer, and medieval drama. Detailed bibliographic footnotes are revised and extended in the bibliographic supplement, including checklists of critical studies on the *Pearl* poet, Langland, and Chaucer.

A217   Renwick, W[illiam] L[indsay] and Harold Orton. *The Beginnings of English Literature to Skelton, 1509.* 3rd ed. rev. by Martyn F. Wakelin. London: Cresset Pr., 1966. (Dobrée, *Introductions to English Literature*, vol. 1)

Contains a general introductory chapter and a good annotated bibliography, pp. 116-486, including both language and literature and providing reading lists for many minor authors and for *Beowulf*, Chaucer, Malory, Gower, Langland, the *Pearl* poet, Skelton, and for Scottish literature of the period.

A218   Zesmer, David M. *Guide to English Literature: From Beowulf Through Chaucer and Medieval Drama.* N.Y.: Barnes and Noble, 1961.

Includes scholarly introductions to all of Chaucer's *Canterbury Tales*, as well as *Piers Plowman, Beowulf*, the Arthurian romances, and works of the *Pearl* poet. Contains a carefully annotated bibliography by Stanley B. Greenfield (A47-48).

VII:1:b:ii RENAISSANCE (1500-1660)

A219 Brooke, Tucker and Matthias A. Shaaber. *The Renaissance* (*1500-1660*). 2nd ed. N.Y.: Appleton-Century-Crofts, 1967. (Baugh, *A Literary History of England*, vol. 2)

> Chapters on Sidney and the Sonneteers, Spenser, Marlowe, Shakespeare, Jacobean drama, Bacon, and Milton.

A220 Bush, Douglas. *English Literature in the Earlier Seventeenth Century, 1600-1660*. 2nd ed. rcv. Oxford: Clarendon Pr., 1962. (*OHEL*, vol. 5)

> Contains information on songbooks and miscellanies, the literature of travel, political, scientific, and religious thought, heroic verse and Milton, with a good bibliography revised to 1961, pp. 461-668.

A221 Lewis, C[live] S[taples]. *English Literature in the Sixteenth Century Excluding Drama.* Oxford: Clarendon Pr., 1954. (*OHEL*, vol. 3)

> Divides the period into "drab" verse and transitional prose and the "golden" period of Sidney and Spenser. Selected bibliography, pp. 594-685.

A222 Pinto, V[ivian] de Sola. *The English Renaissance, 1510-1688.* 3rd rev. ed. London: Cresset Pr., 1966. (Dobrée, *Introductions to English Literature*, vol. 2)

> Social, historical and philosophic background on the renaissance, the Elizabethans, and the seventeenth century, with a chapter on literature and music by Bruce Pattison, pp. 104-129. Annotated bibliography entitled "Students' Guide to Reading," pp. 133-394.

VII:1:b:iii RESTORATION AND THE EIGHTEENTH CENTURY (1660-1800)

A223 Dobrée, Bonamy. *English Literature in the Early Eighteenth Century, 1700-1740.* Oxford: Clarendon Pr., 1959. (*OHEL*, vol. 7)

> Detailed chapters on Defoe, Swift, and Pope, and general chapters on the poets, dramatists, essayists, and controversialists of the period. Background information on letters, memoirs, travel, historians, philosophers, critics, and aestheticians. Selective bibliography, pp. 586-696.

A224   Dyson, H[enry] V[ictor] D[yson] and John Butt. *Augustans and Romantics, 1689-1830.* 3rd rev. ed. London: Cresset Pr., 1961. (Dobrée, *Introductions to English Literature,* vol. 3)

>   Philosophic, economic, and aesthetic background on the Augustans, the age of Johnson, and the Romantics. Annotated bibliography, pp. 151-329, on such topics as political pamphleteers, journalism, diaries, and the blue stockings.

A225   McKillop, Alan Dugald. *English Literature from Dryden to Burns.* N.Y.: Appleton-Century-Crofts, 1948. (*Appleton-Century Handbooks of Literature*)

>   A brief critical survey with bio-bibliographies of major figures of the period and a bibliography of general critical studies appended.

A226   Sherburn, George and Donald F. Bond. *The Restoration and Eighteenth Century (1660-1789).* 2nd ed. N.Y.: Appleton - Century - Crofts, 1967. (Baugh, *A Literary History of England,* vol. 3)

>   Chapters on Dryden, Restoration drama, Defoe, Swift, Addison and Steele, Pope, Dr. Johnson, Cowper, and Burns.

A227   Sutherland, James R[uncieman]. *English Literature of the Late Seventeenth Century.* Oxford: Clarendon Pr., 1969. (*OHEL*, vol. 6)

>   Contains general information on Restoration drama, poetry, and prose fiction as well as biography, history, the literature of travel, and background information on religions, politics, economics, and philosophy of the time. Bibliography, pp. 442-578.

VII:1:b:iv   NINETEENTH CENTURY

A228   Batho, Edith C[lara] and Bonamy Dobrée. *The Victorians and After, 1830-1914.* 3rd ed. rev. London: Cresset Pr., 1962. (Dobrée, *Introductions to English Literature,* vol. 4)

>   General literary background with a chapter by Guy Chapman on the economic background, and brief checklists of the authors works, pp. 132-356.

A229 Bernbaum, Ernest. *Guide through the Romantic Movement.*
2nd ed. rev. and enl. N.Y.: Ronald Pr., 1949.

> A detailed outline history with separate chapters on in-
> dividual authors and a selected bibliography at the end of
> each chapter.

A230 Chew, Samuel C[laggett] and Richard D[aniel] Altick. *The
Nineteenth Century and After (1789-1939)*. 2nd ed.
N.Y.: Appleton-Century-Crofts, 1967. (Baugh, *A Liter-
ary History of England*, vol. 4)

> Chapters on the Romantic and Victorian poets, the
> Victorian novelists, Carlyle, Ruskin, the Pre-Raphaelites,
> the late Victorian poets, modern drama, novel, and poetry.

A231 Cooke, John D[aniel] and Lionel Stevenson. *English Literature of the Victorian Period*. N.Y.: Appleton-Century-
Crofts, 1949. (*Appleton-Century Handbooks of Literature*)

> Contains bio-bibliographies of the major figures of the
> Victorian era.

A232 Jack, Ian [Robert] [James]. *English Literature, 1815-1832.*
Oxford: Clarendon Pr., 1963. (*OHEL*, vol. 10)

> Separate chapters on Byron, Shelley, Keats, Clare and
> the minor poets, the Waverley romances, Peacock, John
> Galt and the minor writers of prose fiction, Hazlitt, Lamb,
> De Quincey, miscellaneous prose, and background infor-
> mation on history, biography, and autobiography. Se-
> lective bibliography, pp. 458-631.

A233 Parrott, Thomas Marc and Robert Bernard Martin. *A
Companion to Victorian Literature*. N.Y.: Scribner's,
1955.

> Brief biographical introductions to the major figures of the
> period with a listing of primary and secondary sources
> appended.

A234 Renwick, W[illiam] L[indsay]. *English Literature, 1789-
1815*. Oxford: Clarendon Pr., 1963. (*OHEL*, vol. 9)

> Contains background information on social, political,
> and scientific aspects of the age, with a selected bibliog-
> raphy pp. 254-289, covering such authors as Austen,

Blake, Coleridge, Lamb, Landor, Monk Lewis, Sir Walter Scott, Southey, and Wordsworth.

See also: Dyson and Butt, *Augustans and Romantics* (A224).

VII:1:b:v TWENTIETH CENTURY

A235   Daiches, David. *The Present Age, After 1920*. London: Cresset Pr., 1958. (Dobrée, *Introductions to English Literature*, vol. 5)

General background on Yeats, the Georgians, Eliot, Auden, modern fiction, critical and general prose, and drama. Brief checklists of the authors' writings, pp. 171-368.

A236   Longaker, J[ohn] Mark and Edwin C. Bolles. *Contemporary English Literature*. N.Y.: Appleton-Century-Crofts, 1953. (*Appleton-Century Handbooks of Literature*)

Author bibliographies.

A237   Millet, Fred B[enjamin]. *Contemporary British Literature: A Critical Survey and 232 Author Bibliographies*. 3rd rev. and enl. ed. by John M. Manly and Edith Rickert. N.Y.: Harcourt, Brace, 1935.

Major writers born after 1850. Contains a selected bibliography of social, political, and literary history, pp. 525-529.

A238   Stewart, J[ohn] I[nnes] M[acintosh]. *Eight Modern Writers*. Oxford: Clarendon Pr., 1963. (*OHEL*, vol. 12)

Separate chapters on Hardy, James, Shaw, Conrad, Kipling, Yeats, Joyce, and Lawrence with a selective bibliography, pp. 629-694.

VII:2 AMERICAN LITERATURE

A239   Spiller, Robert E. [and others], eds. *Literary History of the United States*. 3rd ed. rev. N.Y.: Macmillan, 1963. (*LHUS* or Spiller)

Standard history, containing the basic and most comprehensive bibliography of American literature. See A27.

A240   Millet, Fred B[enjamin]. *Contemporary American Authors: A Critical Survey and 219 Bio-Bibliographies.* N.Y.: Harcourt, Brace, 1943.

> Contains biographies and bibliographies (books and articles) of American authors between 1900 and 1939, and a critical survey of the novel, short story, drama, theatre, and poetry.

A241   Taylor, Walter Fuller. *The Story of American Letters.* Rev. ed. Chicago: Harry Regnery Co., 1956.

> The best general literary survey of American literature, with a brief bibliography, pp. 483-490.

VII:3 CANADIAN LITERATURE

A242   Klinck, Carl F[rederick] [and others], eds. *Literary History of Canada: Canadian Literature in English.* Toronto: University of Toronto Pr., 1965.

> Standard work, presenting both historical and critical examination of writing in Canada, and including bibliography, pp 853-867.

A243   Pacey, Desmond. *Creative Writing in Canada: A Short History of English-Canadian Literature.* 2nd ed. Toronto: Ryerson Pr., 1961.

> An excellent survey, with suggestions for further reading, including articles on individual authors, pp. 283-300.

VII:4 DRAMA AND THEATRE

VII:4:a   GENERAL

A244   Nicoll, Allardyce. *A History of English Drama, 1660-1959.* Rev. ed. Cambridge: Cambridge University Pr., 1955-1959. 6 vols.

> The standard history covering the various genres of the drama, the audience, the theatres, the actors, actresses, and managers from the Restoration to the end of the

nineteenth century. Vol. 6 is a short-title alphabetical catalogue of plays produced or printed in England from 1660 to 1900. Vols. 1-5 of this series are individually itemized in section VII:4:b.

A245   ———. *British Drama: An Historical Survey from the Beginnings to the Present Time.* 5th ed. London: Harrap, 1962.

An excellent survey from the earliest times to the thirties and forties of the twentieth century.

VII:4:b   PERIOD

A246   Chambers, E[dmund] K[erchever]. *The Medieval Stage.* Oxford: Clarendon Pr., 1903. 2 vols.

Standard background study on the origins of play-acting in England and its development during the Middle Ages with information on minstrelsy, folk drama, religious plays, and the interlude.

A247   ———. *The Elizabethan Stage.* Oxford: Clarendon Pr., 1923. 4 vols.

A standard study covering playhouses, companies, playwrights, bibliographies of extant and lost plays, and all other aspects of the Elizabethan stage, ending at the death of Shakespeare. Out-of-date, but still valuable.

A248   Wilson F[rank] P[ercy]. *The English Drama, 1485-1585.* Ed. with a bibliography by G. K. Hunter. Oxford: Clarendon Pr., 1969. (*OHEL*, vol. 4, pt. 1)

Chapters on the Tudor dramatists, masques, pageants, sacred drama, comedy and tragedy, with a selective bibliography, pp. 202-237, covering literary histories, collections, particular studies, individual authors, and anonymous plays.

A249   Wickham, Glynne [William] [Gladstone]. *Early English Stages: 1300 to 1660.* London: Routledge and Kegan Paul, 1959-. 2 vols.

In progress. Especially useful for the physical characteristics of the stage from the beginnings to the establishment of the proscenium arch. Also presents much evidence challenging the received history of English drama.

A250   Bentley, Gerald Eades. *The Jacobean and Caroline Stage.* Oxford: Clarendon Pr., 1941-1968. 7 vols.

> Continues Chambers' *The Elizabethan Stage* (A247) from 1616 to the closing of the theatres in 1642. Includes biographies of actors, histories of companies, bio-bibliographies of the playwrights, and bibliographical-critical notes on some 1200 plays.

A251   Nicoll, Allardyce, *Restoration Drama: 1660-1700.* 4th ed. Cambridge: Cambridge University Pr., 1955. (In his *A History of English Drama 1660-1900*, vol. 1)

> General background information on the theatre and special sections on tragedy and comedy with individual chapters on Shadwell, Mrs. Behn, and Dryden.

A252   ———. *Early Eighteenth Century Drama.* 3rd ed. Cambridge: Cambridge University Pr., 1955. (In his *A History of English Drama 1660-1900*, vol. 2)

> Contains information on such topics as the heroic dramas and various types of tragedies, the Augustan comedy (comedies of manners, etc.), and miscellaneous forms of drama (tragi-comedies and pastorals, ballud - operas, masques, political plays, and burlesques).

A253   ———. *Late Eighteenth Century Drama 1750-1800.* [2nd ed.] Cambridge: Cambridge University Pr., 1955. (In his *A History of English Drama 1660-1900*, vol. 3)

> Contains information on sentimental comedy, the comedy of manners, and the comedy of humours and of intrigue, as well as tragedy and miscellaneous forms of drama.

A254   ———. *Early Nineteenth Century Drama: 1800-1850.* [2nd ed.] Cambridge: Cambridge University Pr., 1955. (In his *A History of English Drama 1660-1900*, vol. 4)

> Background information on dramatic conditions of the age and melodramas, farces, burlesques, as well as tragedies and comedies.

A255   ———. *Late Nineteenth Century Drama: 1850-1900.* [2nd ed.] Cambridge: Cambridge University Pr., 1959. (In his *A History of English Drama 1660-1900*, vol. 5)

> General background information and special chapters on

Boucicault and Taylor, Robertson and Byron, Gilbert and Albery, Jones and Pinero, Wilde and Shaw.

See also: *MHRA* (A5) for a section entitled: "Literature, General: Drama and Theatre History."

VII:5 NOVEL

A256 Baker, Ernest A[lbert]. *History of the English Novel.* London: Witherby, 1924-1939. 10 vols.

> Standard history of the development of English novel and the influences upon it. Individual chapters on the major writers of prose fiction from Chrétien de Troyes to D. H. Lawrence.

A257 Allen, Walter E[rnest]. *The English Novel: A Short Critical History.* London: Phoenix House, 1954.

> A survey of the novel from approximately 1670 to the work of James Joyce and D. H. Lawrence.

See also: *MHRA* (A5) for a section entitled: "Literature, General: Fiction."

VII:6 POETRY

A258 Courthope, W[illiam] J[ohn]. *A History of English Poetry.* London: Macmillan, 1895-1910. 6 vols.

> Detailed history from medieval poetry to the Romantic movement.

A259 Grierson, Herbert J. C. and J[ohn] C[lifford] Smith. *A Critical History of English Poetry.* 2nd ed. London: Chatto and Windus, 1947.

> Good survey from Anglo-Saxon poetry to the twentieth century.

See also: *MHRA* (A5) for a section entitled: "Literature, General: Poetry."

VIII

AUXILIARY SUBJECTS

VIII:1 LANGUAGE, LINGUISTICS, STYLE, AND RHETORIC

For topics of wide scope, additional information may be found under a wide variety of subject headings in the card catalogue. Since linguistics is a relatively new field, many new headings have been added in the supplements to the seventh edition of the Library of Congress list of subject headings. Some of these new headings are: Linguistics; Sociolinguistics; Structural Linguistics. Consult also such headings as: Grammar, Comparative and General; Mathematical Linguistics; Phonetics; English Language—Morphology; American Language—Semantics. For style and rhetoric consult: Aureate Terms; English Language—Rhetoric; Style, Literary.

A260   Allen, Harold B[yron], comp. *Linguistics and English Linguistics.* N.Y.: Appleton-Century-Crofts, 1966. (*Goldentree Bibliographies*)

> A convenient guide to linguistic scholarship. Excludes articles on current British English unless they have some relevance to American English. Includes references to articles on Canadian English.

A261   Alston, R[obin] C. *A Bibliography of the English Language from the Invention of Printing to the Year 1800.* Leeds: E. J. Arnold and Son, 1965-

> To be in 20 vols., 8 vols. published to date. Eventually will supersede Kennedy (A268) for material published up to 1800. Volumes on such topics as English grammars, spelling, the English dictionary, rhetoric, prosody, rhyme, and dialect.

A262   ———, and J. L. Rosier. "Rhetoric and Style: A Bibliographical Guide," *Leeds Studies in English,* I (1967), 137-159.

Contains primary works, as well as books and articles on the classical, medieval, and renaissance traditions, on the theories of style, and on diction, metaphor, prose style, and poetic rhythm.

A263   Bennett, James R. "An Annotated Bibliography of Selected Writings on English Prose Style," *College Composition and Communication*, XVI (1965), 248-255.

Bibliography of books, articles, and dissertations, divided by general periods, with occasional annotations.

A264   ———. "English Prose Style from Alfred to More: A Bibliography," *Medieval Studies*, XXX (1968), 248-259.

Annotated bibliography of articles, books, dissertations, and reviews.

A265   ———. "Style in Twentieth Century British and American Fiction: A Bibliography," *West Coast Review*, II, No. 3 (1968), 43-51.

Annotated bibliography of books, articles, and dissertations, listed by individual authors.

A266   Brenni, Vito J[oseph], comp. *American English: A Bibliography*. Philadelphia: University of Pennsylvania Pr., 1964.

Annotated bibliography on history, grammar, syntax, usage, pronunciation, slang and dialects, listing articles, books, and dissertations.

A267   Cleary, J[ames] W[illiam] and F[rederick] W. Haberman, eds. *Rhetoric and Public Address: A Bibliography, 1947-1961*. Madison: University of Wisconsin Pr., 1964.

Comprehensive listing of important publications from 1947-1961. Includes articles, books, monographs, reviews, and dissertations on style and rhetoric.

A268   Kennedy, Arthur G[arfield]. *A Bibliography of Writings on the English Language, from the Beginning of Printing to the End of 1922*. Cambridge, Mass.: Harvard University Pr., 1927.

Still the only full-length bibliography on the subject. Articles and books on the use of language by individual authors of all periods and general studies on the history, theory, grammar, and dialects of language. Alston (A261) will eventually supersede Kennedy, for material published up to 1800.

A269 Milic, Louis T[onka]. *Style and Stylistics: An Analytical Bibliography*. N.Y.: Free Pr., 1967.

Includes many books and articles on the style of individual authors as well as on theoretical and methodological aspects of the study of style.

A270 Rice, Frank [A.] and Allene Guss, eds. *Information Sources in Linguistics: A Bibliographical Handbook*. Washington, D.C.: Center for Applied Linguistics, 1965.

Covers the reference material in all the major fields of linguistics and related disciplines. Excludes works treating individual languages. For individual languages see *Bibliographie linguistique* (A273).

A271 Scheurweghs, G[ustave]. *Analytical Bibliography of Writings on Modern English Morphology and Syntax, 1877-1960*. Louvain, Belgium: Publications of the University of Louvain, 1963-1968. 4 vols.

Comprehensive, concisely annotated listing of books, articles, and dissertations treating all aspects of English syntax and morphology as the language developed from the 16th Century to the present. Includes works by Japanese and Eastern European authors.

A272 Steible, Daniel J. *Concise Handbook of Linguistics: A Glossary of Terms*. N.Y.: Philosophical Library, 1967.

Intended for the student of English linguistics, offering brief, simplified explanations of terms in widespread use by linguists and teachers of linguistics.

A273 *Bibliographie linguistique*. 1939/47-. Utrecht: Permanent International Committee of Linguists, 1949-

Standard annual bibliography listing books, reviews, and articles in all languages in various branches of linguistics, including phonetics, grammar, history of language, linguistic geography and dialectology, vocabulary, stylistics, prosody, mathematical linguistics, and philosophy, psychology, and sociology of language. Contains also separate sections on the individual languages of all language families.

A274   "Annual Bibliography," 1966-

> Published annually in *Style* since 1967. Emphasis is on essays dealing with the language of literature; covers articles, books, Festschriften, dissertations, some foreign language material.

A275   "Linguistica Canadiana," 1955-

> Published annually in *The Canadian Journal of Linguistics* since 1956, containing critical articles on languages prevalent in Canada.

The Linguistics Division of *PMLA* (A15) has many subsections. For example: *General Linguistics* covers Mathematical and Computational Linguistics, Information and Communication Theory, Stylistics, Study of Meaning, Psycholinguistics, Socio- and Ethnolinguistics, Dialectology. *Theoretical and Descriptive Linguistics* covers Phonology, Prosody, Philosophy of Language. There are also sections entitled: "Comparative and Historical Linguistics", "Indo-European Linguistics: English."

See also: *MHRA* (A5) for sections entitled: "Language, General," "The Sounds of Speech," "Dictionaries and Grammars," "Vocabulary," and "Syntax."

Wellek and Warren, *Theory of Literature* (A303).

VIII:2 COMPARATIVE LITERATURE

(Including the relation of literature to other fields)

For topics of wide scope, consult the subject section of the card catalogue under such headings as: Art and Literature; Music and Literature; Literature, Comparative; Literature and Science; Psychology in Literature.

A276   Baldensperger, F[ernand] and Werner P. Friederich. *Bibliography of Comparative Literature*. N.Y.: Russell and Russell, 1960.

> Covers literary themes (fables and fabliaux, sagas, myths and mythology, collective motifs) and the influence of all

literatures on English literature in general and on individual authors. Brought up-to-date by the *Yearbook of
Comparative and General Literature* (A285).

A277   Kiell, Norman, ed. *Psychoanalysis, Psychology, and Literature: A Bibliography*. Madison: University of Wisconsin
Pr., 1963.

Over 4,000 entries covering the period 1900-1961 with a
subject index. Articles on such topics as death in literature,
symbolism, the dream, and on individual author's works.

A278   Modern Language Association of America. General Topics
IX. *A Bibliography on the Relations of Literature and
Other Arts, 1952-1967*. N.Y.: New York Public Library,
1968.

Covers the relationship of literature to both music and
the visual arts. Includes articles and books, and indexes
some foreign language journals. Contains an author index.

A279   ———. General Topics VI. *Literature and Society: A
Selective Bibliography*. 1950/55-. Coral Gables, Fla.:
University of Miami Pr., 1956-

Selects books and articles providing some literary expression of history, sociology, philosophy, religion, political science, folklore, aesthetics, psychology, publishing,
and communication. Emphasis is on the novel and novelists,
and the bulk of journals indexed are American. Three
cumulations issued at 5-year intervals extend the coverage
to 1965.

A280   Singer, Armand E[dwards]. *The Don Juan Theme, Versions
and Criticism: A Bibliography*. Morgantown: West Virginia University, 1965.

Criticism on individual works of Browning, Byron, Shaw,
and others.

A281   Thorpe, James [Ernest], ed. *Relations of Literary Study:
Essays on Interdisciplinary Contributions*. N.Y.: Modern
Language Association of America, 1967.

Contains essays on the relationship of literature to history,
myth, biography, psychology, sociology, religion, and
music with bibliographical footnotes and selected bibliographies on Literature and Myth by Northrop Frye,

pp. 43-55; Literature and Biography, by Leon Edel, p. 71; Literature and Sociology, by Leo Lowenthal, pp. 100-110; Literature and Music, by Bertrand Bronson, pp. 149-150.

A282   Vowles, Richard B. "Psychology and Drama: A Selected Checklist," *Wisconsin Studies in Contemporary Literature*, III, No. 1 (1962), 35-48.

> Divided by individual authors. Reviews the research between 1920 and 1961.

A283   "Bibliography," 1964/65-

> An annotated listing, published annually as a supplement to *Literature and Psychology* since 1967. Journals indexed are mainly American.

A284   "Relations of Literature and Science: A Selected Bibliography," 1950-

> Published annually in *Symposium* since 1951 on behalf of General Topics VII of the Modern Language Association. Contains books and articles on the relationship between literature and botany, astronomy, medicine, anthropology, and psychology. A compilation has been issued: Dudley, Fred A., ed. *The Relations of Literature and Science: A Selected Bibliography, 1930-1967*. Ann Arbor, Mich.: University Microfilms, 1968.

A285   *Yearbook of Comparative and General Literature*. Chapel Hill: University of North Carolina Pr., 1952-

> Annual bibliography of scholarly and critical works in comparative literature; annual lists of translations into English.

See also: *PMLA* (A15) for a section entitled: "General Literature and Related Topics: Literature, General and Comparative; Themes and Types."

Pinto, *The English Renaissance, 1510-1688* (A222), pp. 104-129.

Wellek and Warren, *Theory of Literature* (A303).

VIII:3 MYTH, FOLKLORE, AND SYMBOLISM

For topics of wide scope, much additional information may be found under a wide variety of subject headings in the card catalogue. For mythology, consult such headings as: Mythology, Classical; Mythology in Literature. For folklore and symbolism, consult such headings as: Folk Literature—Themes, Motives; Folk-lore of Birds; Love in Literature; Flowers in Literature; Fire (in Religion, Folklore, etc.); Christian Art and Symbolism; Symbolism of Numbers.

A286   Bulfinch, Thomas. *Mythology: The Age of Fable; The Age of Chivalry; Legends of Charlemagne.* N.Y.: Crowell, 1959.

> Standard reference work since the m i d d l e of the nineteenth century.

A287   Bush, Douglas. *Mythology and the Renaissance Tradition in English Poetry.* New rev. ed. N.Y.: Norton, 1963.
> Includes special studies on Spenser, Marlowe, Shakespeare, Drayton, Milton, and other more obscure figures, with a bibliography of articles and books, pp. 340-353, and an appendix containing a list of mythological poems up to 1680, pp. 311-339.

A288   ———. *Mythology and the Romantic Tradition in English Poetry.* Cambridge, Mass.: Harvard University Pr., 1937.

> Continues A287 from the eighteenth century to the present, with special chapters on major Romantic and Victorian poets and American poets. Includes also a bibliography of books and articles, pp. 596-627, and an appendix containing an extensive list of mythological poems, 1680 to the present, pp. 539-592.

A289   Cirlot, J[uan] E[duardo]. *A Dictionary of Symbols.* Tr. Jack Sage. N.Y.: Philosophical Library, 1962.

> A guide to major symbols in mythology, religion, psychology, music, art, and literature. Entries on the Tarot pack, water, colour, the serpent, numbers, and the cross.

A290   Eliade, Mircea. *Images and Symbols: Studies in Religious Symbolism.* Tr. Philip Mairet. London: Harvill Pr., 1961.

        Not designed as a reference work, but useful as a supplementary source.

A291   Frazer, Sir James George. *The Golden Bough: A Study in Magic and Religion.* 3rd ed. London: Macmillan, 1911-15. 12 vols.

        Standard work, containing a detailed index.

A292   Gray, Louis Herbert, ed. *The Mythology of All Races.* Boston: Marshall Jones, 1916. 13 vols.

        The most comprehensive reference work on mythology. Contains a detailed, analytical index.

A293   Jobes, Gertrude. *Dictionary of Mythology, Folklore and Symbols.* N.Y.: Scarecrow Pr., 1961. 3 vols.

        Very comprehensive, i n c l u d i n g Oriental and North American mythology, and providing an excellent key to conventional symbols in the history of ideas. Contains many more entries than Cirlot (A289).

A294   *The Oxford Companion to Classical Literature.* Ed. Sir Paul Harvey. Oxford: Clarendon Pr., 1937.

        Contains concise information about classical writers and their works and on the historical, religious, and social background. Points out relationships between classical literature and medieval and modern English Literature.

A295   *The Oxford Classical Dictionary.* Oxford: Clarendon Pr., 1949.

        Concludes with the death of Constantine, 337 A.D. Christian writers are excluded, although a few prominent figures of later ages, such as Augustine, are included.

A296   Thompson, Stith. *Motif-Index of Folk-Literature.* Copenhagen: Rosenkilde and Bagger, 1956. 6 vols.

        Classifies narrative elements in folktales, ballads, myths, fables, medieval romances, exempla, fabliaux, jest-books, and local legends. Specific references to standard works on mythology, including *Mythology of All Races* (A292).

A297 *Internationale volkskundliche Bibliographie,* 1939/41-. Bonn: Rudolf Habelt Verlag, 1949-

> Called *Volkskundliche Bibliographie,* 1939-1954. Standard annual bibliography for folklore, containing sections on mythology, English folk poetry, legends, and history of themes and motifs. Approximately 4 years time lag.

See also: *MHRA* (A5) for a section entitled: "Ancillary Studies: Mythology, Legend, Folk-Lore."

PMLA (A15) for a section entitled: "General Literature and Related Topics: Themes and Types; Folklore."

Brewer, *Dictionary of Phrase and Fable* (A154).

Sanders, *An Introduction to Research in English Literary History* (A181), pp. 253-276.

Stallman, "A Selected Bibliography of Criticism on Modern Fiction" (A104), pp. 570-572.

Thorpe, *Relations of Literary Study* (A281), pp. 43-55.

Wellck and Warren, *Theory of Literature* (A303).

VIII:4 AESTHETICS AND HISTORY OF CRITICISM

For topics of wide scope, consult the subject section of the card catalogue under such headings as: Aesthetics; Criticism-History; Naturalism in Literature; Romanticism.

A298 Leary, Lewis G[aston]. *Contemporary Literary Scholarship: A Critical Review.* N.Y.: Appleton-Century-Crofts, 1958.

> A critical survey of scholarship in all periods and genres; each chapter by a specialist. A bibliography at the end lists some 50 critical works published in the last 30 years which were regarded as the best contributions to the understanding of literature.

A299   Stallman, Robert Wooster, ed. "A Selected Bibliography of Modern Criticism: 1920-1948," in his *Critiques and Essays in Criticism*. N.Y.: Ronald Pr., 1949, pp. 519-571.

> Includes books, essays, reviews, and symposia, both British and American, in the fields of scholarship and the history of criticism, poetry, fiction, aesthetics, art (painting and music), and related works.

A300   Sutton, Walter [E.]. *Modern American Criticism*. Englewood Cliffs, N.J.: Prentice-Hall, 1963. (*Princeton Studies, Humanistic Scholarship in America*)

> A compact survey of the last five decades of literary criticism in the U.S., restricted largely to American literature. No separate bibliography, but a good index of critics.

A301   Watson, George. *The Literary Critics: A Study of English Descriptive Criticism*. Baltimore: Penguin Books, 1962.

> Surveys the criticism of Dryden, Pope, Addison, Fielding, Dr. Johnson, Wordsworth and Coleridge, Lamb, Hazlitt, De Quincey, Arnold, James, T. S. Eliot, I. A. Richards, William Empson, and F. R. Leavis, with a select bibliography of modern editions and studies, pp. 228-237.

A302   Wellek, René. *A History of Modern Criticism: 1750-1950*. London: Jonathan Cape, 1955-

> 4 vols. published to date. Vol. 5 to cover the twentieth century. Standard work covering the later eighteenth century, the Romantic age, the age of transition and the later nineteenth century. Contains detailed bibliographic notes and brief bibliographies on individual authors; some evaluative annotations.

A303   ————, and Austin Warren. *Theory of Literature*. 3rd ed. rev. N.Y.: Harcourt, Brace and World, 1956.

> Contains a thorough bibliography restricted to the last 100 years, pp. 317-357. In addition to literary theory, criticism and history, covers also the relationship of literature to biography, psychology and society, and contains chapters on euphony, rhythm and metre; style and stylistics; image, metaphor, symbol and myth.

A304   Wimsatt, William K[urtz] and Cleanth Brooks. *Literary Criticism: A Short History*. N.Y.: Knopf, 1957.

Contains detailed bibliographic footnotes. Surveys criticism from Plato and Aristotle to the present day, covering both English and American criticism, and including articles, essays, and books.

A305   "Current Literature: II. Criticism and Biography," 1934-

A survey published annually in *English Studies* since 1935.

A306   "Selective Current Bibliography for Aesthetics and Related Fields," Jan. 1945-

Published intermittently in *Journal of Aesthetics and Art Criticism* from Dec. 1945 to June 1947, then annually in the June issue. Contains sections entitled "General Aesthetics and Philosophy of Art" and "Literature."

See also: *MHRA* (A5) for a section entitled: "Literature, General: Literary Criticism."

PMLA (A15) for a section entitled: "General Literature and Related Topics: Aesthetics; Literary Criticism and Literary Theory."

Fleischmann, *Encyclopedia of World Literature in the 20th Century* (A145), vol. 2, pp. 326-328.

VIII:5   SOCIAL AND INTELLECTUAL HISTORY

This is a highly selective listing of social and intellectual histories. Many more can be found in the card catalogue under the following subject headings: Great Britain—History; Great Britain—Social Conditions. Similar headings appear for the United States and Canada.

VIII:5:a   GENERAL

A307   *The Oxford History of England.* Ed. G. N. Clark. Oxford: Clarendon Pr., 1937-. 15 vols.

Standard history, containing background information useful to the student of literature. Individual volumes are separately itemized in section VIII:5:b.

A308   Trevelyan G[eorge] M[acaulay]. *English Social History: A Survey of Six Centuries, Chaucer to Queen Victoria.* London: Longmans, 1943.

   Excellent introductory survey.

VIII:5:b   PERIOD

VIII:5:b:i   ANGLO-SAXON

A309   Collingwood, R[obin] G[eorge] and J. L. N. Myres. *Roman Britain and the English Settlements.* 2nd ed. Oxford: Clarendon Pr., 1937. (*The Oxford History of England,* vol. 1)

A310   Hodgkin, R[obert] H[oward]. *A History of the Anglo-Saxons.* 3rd ed. London: Oxford University Pr., 1940. 2 vols.

A311   Stenton, F[rank] M[erry]. *Anglo-Saxon England.* 2nd ed. Oxford: Clarendon Pr., 1947. (*The Oxford History of England,* vol. 2)

VIII:5:b:ii   MIDDLE AGES

A312   Coulton, G[eorge] G[ordon]. *Medieval Panorama: The English Scene from Conquest to Reformation.* N.Y.: Meridian Bks., 1938.

   A standard survey providing background information on such topics as nature and superstition, chivalry, the monastery, cloister life, the Lollards, the Black Death, and women's life.

A313   Jacob, E[rnest] F[raser]. *The Fifteenth Century, 1399-1485.* Oxford: Clarendon Pr., 1961. (*The Oxford History of England,* vol. 6)

A314   Jusserand, J[ean] [Adrien] [Antoine] J[ules]. *English Wayfaring Life in the Middle Ages.* 4th ed. London: Ernest Benn, 1950.

   Introductory background on both lay and religious wayfarers.

A315 McKisack, May. *The Fourteenth Century, 1307-1399*. Oxford: Clarendon Pr., 1959. (*The Oxford History of England*, vol. 5)

A316 Poole, Austin Lane. *From Domesday Book to Magna Carta, 1087-1216*. 2nd ed. Oxford: Clarendon Pr., 1955 (*The Oxford History of England*, vol. 3)

A317 ———, ed. *Medieval England*. New ed. rewr. and rev. Oxford: Clarendon Pr., 1958. 2 vols.

> A general, well-illustrated survey with chapters on "Religious Life and Organizations" and "Towns and Trade." Omits feudalism and government, emphasizing instead cultural history.

A318 Powicke, Sir [Frederick] Maurice. *The Thirteenth Century, 1216-1307*. 2nd ed. Oxford: Clarendon Pr., 1962. (*The Oxford History of England*, vol. 4)

VIII:5:b:iii
SIXTEENTH AND SEVENTEENTH CENTURIES

A319 Black J[ohn] B[ennett]. *The Reign of Elizabeth, 1558-1603*. 2nd ed. Oxford: Clarendon Pr., 1959. (*The Oxford History of England*, vol. 8)

A320 Clark, Sir George [Norman]. *The Later Stuarts, 1660-1740*. 2nd ed. Oxford: Clarendon Pr., 1955. (*The Oxford History of England*, vol. 10)

A321 Davies, Godfrey. *The Early Stuarts, 1603-1660*. 2nd ed. Oxford: Clarendon Pr., 1959. (*The Oxford History of England*, vol. 9)

A322 Mackie, J[ohn] D[uncan]. *The Earlier Tudors, 1485-1558*. Oxford: Clarendon Pr., 1952. (*The Oxford History of England*, vol. 7)

A323 *Shakespeare's England: An Account of the Life and Manners of His Age*. Oxford: Clarendon Pr., 1916. 2 vols.

> Each chapter by a specialist with a bibliography appended; includes information on folklore and superstitions, medi-

cine, law, religion, science, the court, ballads, and broad-
sides, and Shakespeare's English.

A324   Tillyard, E[ustace] M[andeville] W[etenhall]. *The Elizabethan World Picture.* London: Chatto and Windus,
1943.

> Excellent introduction to the philosophy, religion, and
> political theories of the period, including chapters on
> order, sin, and the chain of being.

A325   Willey, Basil. *The Seventeenth Century Background: Studies
in the Thought of the Age in Relation to Poetry and
Religion.* London: Chatto and Windus, 1934.

> Background on the idea of 'truth' in Browne, Bacon, and
> Milton, with chapters on Hobbes, the Cambridge Platon-
> ists, and Locke.

VIII:5:b:iv   EIGHTEENTH CENTURY

A326   Turberville, A[rthur] S[tanley], ed. *Johnson's England: An
Account of the Life and Manners of His Age.* Oxford:
Clarendon Pr., 1933. 2 vols.

> Each chapter by a specialist; covers the newspaper, drama
> and the theatre, the theory of taste, education, science,
> and law, and includes bibliographical footnotes.

A327   Watson, J[ohn] Steven. *The Reign of George III, 1760-
1815.* Oxford: Clarendon Pr., 1960. (*The Oxford History of England*, vol. 12)

A328   Willey, Basil. *The Eighteenth Century Background: Studies
on the Idea of Nature in the Thought of the Period.*
London: Chatto and Windus, 1940.

> Introductory background on the idea of 'Nature' in re-
> ligion, ethics, philosophy, and politics, and in particular,
> the divinization of 'Nature' which culminates in Words-
> worth.

A329   Williams, Basil. *The Whig Supremacy, 1714-1760.* 2nd ed.
rev. by C. H. Stuart. Oxford: Clarendon Pr., 1962. (*The
Oxford History of England*, vol. 11)

VIII:5:b:v   NINETEENTH CENTURY

A330   Ensor, R[obert] C[harles] K[irkwood]. *England, 1870-1914*. Oxford: Clarendon Pr., 1936. (*The Oxford History of England*, vol. 14)

A331   Houghton, Walter E[dwards]. *The Victorian Frame of Mind: 1830-1870*. New Haven, Conn.: Yale University Pr., 1957.

> Discusses the emotional, intellectual, and moral attitudes of the age. Contains detailed bibliographic footnotes.

A332   Willey, Basil. *Nineteenth Century Studies: Coleridge to Matthew Arnold*. London: Chatto and Windus, 1949.

> Preliminary study on the history of religious and moral ideas in the nineteenth century, studying the thought of Coleridge, Arnold, Newman, Carlyle, Bentham, Mill, Comte, and George Eliot.

A333   ———. *More Nineteenth Century Studies: A Group of Honest Doubters*. London: Chatto and Windus, 1956.

> Illustrates some phases of Victorian thought through a group of historians, theologians, and men of letters.

A334   Woodward, E[rnest] L[lewellyn]. *The Age of Reform, 1815-1870*. Oxford: Clarendon Pr., 1938. (*The Oxford History of England*, vol. 13)

A335   Young, G[eorge] M[alcolm], ed. *Early Victorian England, 1830-1865*. London: Oxford University Pr., 1934. 2 vols. Written to continue *Shakespeare's England* (A323) and *Johnson's England* (A326).

> Final chapter published as: Young, G[eorge] M[alcolm]. *Victorian England: Portrait of an Age*. 2nd ed. London: Oxford University Pr., 1953.

VIII:5:b:vi   TWENTIETH CENTURY

A336   Hearnshaw, F[ossey] J[ohn] C[obb], ed. *Edwardian England, A.D. 1901-1910*. London: Ernest Benn, 1933.

> Essays on religion, domestic politics, foreign relations, education, literature, science, and political ideas.

A337   Taylor, A[lan] J[ohn] P[ercivale]. *English History, 1914-1945*. Oxford: Clarendon Pr., 1965. (*The Oxford History of England*, vol. 15)

See also: *MHRA* (A5) for a section entitled: "Ancillary Studies: Social History, General."

Section B:

INDIVIDUAL AUTHORS

HOW TO USE THIS SECTION

This section lists secondary bibliographies only. Here the student will find the best available material on each author, rather than an all-inclusive listing. For other authors not found within this section, the student should consult the appropriate general tools within section I:2-4, as well as the index to authors as subjects.

For primary bibliographies, consult:

All authors:	Besterman (A6)
	Bibliographic Index (A7)
British authors:	*CBEL* (A21)
	Howard-Hill (A24)
American authors:	Blanck (A28)
	LHUS (A27)
Canadian authors:	Watters (A39)

For the best available edition of an author's works, consult:

British authors:	Bateson (A22)
Anglo-Saxon authors:	Fisher (A45)
Medieval authors:	Fisher (A45)
Romantic essayists:	Houtchens (A68)
Romantic poets:	Raysor (A69)
	Houtchens (A68)
Victorian novelists:	Stevenson (A76)
Victorian poets:	Faverty (A74)
Nineteenth century American poets:	Stovall (A33)
Twentieth century American writers:	Bryer (A29)

SAMPLE TOPIC I. *Vanity Fair* by Thackeray.

In addition to the items cited within this section under "Thackeray," for a comprehensive bibliography on the topic, also consult:

The Novel (I:4:b)
Victorian Period (I:3:e)
English Literature (I:2:b)
The General Section (I:2:a)

SAMPLE TOPIC II. *The Snows of Kilimanjaro* by Hemingway.

Similarly, for a comprehensive bibliography, consult:
The Short Story (I:4:d)
Twentieth Century (I:3:f)
American Literature (I:2:c)
The General Section (I:2:a)

SAMPLE TOPIC III. *The Waste Land* by T. S. Eliot.

Authors who are born in one country and who publish in another are often claimed by both countries. T. S. Eliot, for example, is considered to be both an American and a British author. For this author, consult:
Poetry (I:4:c)
Twentieth Century (I:3:f)
American Literature (I:2:c)
English Literature (I:2:b)
The General Section (I:2:a)

ALBEE, EDWARD

B1   Kolin, Philip C. "Classified Edward Albee Checklist," *Serif*, VI, No. 3 (1969), 16-32.

B2   Amacher, Richard E. and Margaret Rule. *Edward Albee at Home and Abroad: A Bibliography (1958-June 1968)*. N.Y.: AMS Pr., 1970.

ANDERSON, SHERWOOD

B3   Sheehy, Eugene P[aul] and Kenneth A. Lohf. *Sherwood Anderson: A Bibliography*. Los Gatos, Calif.: Talisman Pr., 1960.

See also: Bryer, *Fifteen Modern American Authors* (A29), pp. 3-22.

ARNOLD, MATTHEW

B4   Smart, Thomas Burnett, comp. *The Bibliography of Matthew Arnold*. N.Y.: Burt Franklin, 1892.

        Updated in Ehrsam, *Twelve Victorian Authors* (A73), pp. 14-45.

See also: Faverty, *The Victorian Poets* (A74), pp. 164-226.

AUDEN, W. H.

B5   Clancy, Joseph. "A W. H. Auden Bibliography 1924-1955," *Thought*, XXX, No. 117 (1955), 260-270.

AUSTEN, JANE

B6   Chapman, R[obert] W[illiam]. *Jane Austen: A Critical Bibliography*. 2nd ed. Oxford: Clarendon Pr., 1955.
        Continued by Link (B7).

B7   Link, Frederick Martin. *The Reputation of Jane Austen in the Twentieth Century with an Annotated Enumerative Bibliography of Austen Criticism from 1811 to June, 1957*. Ph.D. Diss. Boston: Boston University, 1958, pp. 139-369.
        Continues Chapman (B6).

BACON, FRANCIS

B8   Houck, J. Kemp, comp. *Francis Bacon, 1926-1966.* London:
      Nether Pr., 1968. (*Elizabethan Bibliographies Supplements*, 15)

BEAUMONT, FRANCIS

B9   Pennel, Charles A. and William P. Williams, comps. *Francis
      Beaumont, John Fletcher, Philip Massinger, 1937-1965;
      John Ford, 1940-1965; James Shirley, 1945-1965.*
      London: Nether Pr., 1968. (*Elizabethan Bibliographies
      Supplements*, 8)

BECKETT, SAMUEL

B10   Cohn, Ruby. *Samuel Beckett: The Comic Gamut.* New
      Brunswick, N. J.: Rutgers University Pr., 1962, pp. 328-
      340.

B11   Webb, Eugene. "Critical Writings on Samuel Beckett: A
      Bibliography," *West Coast Review*, I, No. 1 (1966),
      56-70.
      Attempts to list as comprehensively as possible the critical
      material that has appeared from 1938 to date.

B12   Tanner, James T. F. and J. Don Vann. *Samuel Beckett: A
      Checklist of Criticism.* Kent, Ohio: Kent State University
      Pr., 1969. (*Serif Series*, 8)

BELLOW, SAUL

B13   Schneider, Harold W. "Two Bibliographies: Saul Bellow
      and William Styron," *Critique*, III, No. 3 (1960), 71-91.
      Continued by Galloway (B14).

B14   Galloway, David D. "A Saul Bellow Checklist" in his *The
      Absurd Hero in American Fiction: Updike, Styron,
      Bellow, Salinger.* Austin: University of Texas Pr., 1966, pp.
      210-226.
      Continues Schneider (B13).

BLAKE, WILLIAM

B15   Bentley, G[erald] E[ades, Jr.] and Martin K. Nurmi. *A Blake
      Bibliography: Annotated Lists of Works, Studies, and*

Blakeana. Minneapolis: University of Minnesota Pr., 1964.
Supplemented by William White in "A Blake Bibliography: Review with Additions," *Bulletin of Bibliography*, XXIV, No. 7 (1965), 155-156.

See also: Houtchens, *The English Romantic Poets and Essayists* (A68), pp. 1-31.

BRONTË, EMILY

B16   Lettis, Richard and William E. Morris. *A Wuthering Heights Handbook.* N.Y.: Odyssey Pr., 1961, pp. 142-144.

See also: Stevenson, *Victorian Fiction* (A76), pp. 214-244.

BRONTË, CHARLOTTE

See: Stevenson, *Victorian Fiction* (A76), pp. 214-244.

BROWNE, SIR THOMAS

B17   Donovan, Dennis G., comp. *Sir Thomas Browne, 1924-1966; Robert Burton, 1924-1966.* London: Nether Pr., 1968. (*Elizabethan Bibliographies Supplements*, 10)

BROWNING, ELIZABETH BARRETT

See: Ehrsam, *Twelve Victorian Authors* (A73), pp. 48-67.

Faverty, *The Victorian Poets* (A74), pp. 121-136.

BROWNING, ROBERT

B18   Broughton, Leslie Nathan, Clark Sutherland Northup and Robert Pearsall, comps. *Robert Browning: A Bibliography, 1830-1950.* Ithaca, N.Y.: Cornell University Pr., 1953. (*Cornell Studies in English*, vol. 39)
Continued by Litzinger (B19).

B19   Litzinger, Boyd and K[enneth] L. Knickerbocker. *The Browning Critics.* Lexington: University of Kentucky Pr., 1961, pp. 391-417.
Continues Broughton (B18).

See also: Faverty, *The Victorian Poets* (A74), pp. 82-120.

BUTLER, SAMUEL

B20 Harkness, Stanley B[ates]. *The Career of Samuel Butler (1835-1902): A Bibliography.* London: Bodley Head, 1955.

BYRON, GEORGE GORDON

B21 Chew, Samuel C[lagett]. *Byron in England: His Fame and After-Fame.* London: John Murray, 1924, pp. 353-407.

See also: Bernbaum, "Keats, Shelley, Byron and Hunt. A Critical Sketch of Important Books and Articles Concerning them Published in 1940-1950" *Keats-Shelley Journal* (B179), pp. 73-85.

Raysor, *The English Romantic Poets* (A69), pp. 138-183.

Singer, *The Don Juan Theme* (A280), pp. 212-223.

CARLYLE, THOMAS

See: Houtchens, *The English Romantic Poets and Essayists* (A68), pp. 333-378.

CATHER, WILLA

B22 Hutchinson, Phyllis Martin. "The Writings of Willa Cather: A List of Works by and About Her, Part III," *New York Public Library Bulletin*, LX, No. 8 (1956), 378-400.

See also: Bryer, *Fifteen Modern American Authors* (A29), pp. 23-62.

CHAUCER, GEOFFREY

B23 Griffith, Dudley David. *Bibliography of Chaucer, 1908-1953.* Seattle: University of Washington Pr., 1955.
Continued by Crawford (B24).

B24 Crawford, William R. *Bibliography of Chaucer, 1954-63.* Seattle: University of Washington Pr., 1967.
Continues Griffith (B23).

B25 Baugh, Albert C[roll], comp. *Chaucer.* N.Y.: Appleton-Century-Crofts, 1968. (*Goldentree Bibliographies*)

B26   "Chaucer Research," 1966-
       Published annually since 1967 in the third issue of *Chaucer Review* and compiled by the M.L.A. Committee on Research and Bibliography, Chaucer Group. Since 1969, published in *Neuphilologische Mitteilungen.*

See also: Fisher, *The Medieval Literature of Western Europe* (A45), pp. 110-122.

CLEMENS, SAMUEL

See: Twain, Mark

CLOUGH, ARTHUR HUGH

See: Ehrsam, *Twelve Victorian Authors* (A73), pp. 68-77.

       Faverty, *The Victorian Poets* (A74), pp. 149-162.

COLERIDGE, SAMUEL TAYLOR

B27   Kennedy, Virginia Wadlow, comp. *Samuel Taylor Coleridge: A Selected Bibliography of the Best Available Editions of his Writings, of Biographies and Criticisms of him, and of References Showing his Relations with Contemporaries.* Baltimore: Enoch Pratt Free Library, 1935.

B28   Hall, Thomas. "A Check List of Coleridge Criticism," *Bulletin of Bibliography,* XXV, No. 5 (1968), 124-131; No. 6, 153-156; No. 7, 175-182.

See also: Raysor, *The English Romantic Poets* (A69), pp. 75-137.

CONRAD, JOSEPH

B29   Beebe, Maurice. "Criticism of Joseph Conrad: A Selected Checklist with an Index to Studies of Separate Works," *Modern Fiction Studies,* I, No. 1 (1955), 30-45; X, No. 1 (1964), 81-106.

B30   Lohf, Kenneth A. and Eugene P. Sheehy. *Joseph Conrad at Mid-Century: Editions and Studies, 1895-1955.* Minneapolis: University of Minnesota Pr., 1957.

B31   Ehrsam, Theodore G[eorge], comp. *A Bibliography of Joseph Conrad*. Metuchen, N.J.: Scarecrow Pr., 1969.

B32   "Bibliography," 1967-

Published in each issue of *Conradiana* since 1968.

COWPER, WILLIAM

B33   Hartley, Lodwick. *William Cowper; the Continuing Revaluation*: *An Essay and a Bibliography of Cowperian Studies from 1895 to 1960*. Chapel Hill: University of North Carolina Pr., 1960, pp. 75-152.

CRANE, HART

B34   Rowe, H. D. "Hart Crane: A Bibliography," *Twentieth Century Literature*, I, No. 2 (1955), 94-113.

Supplemented by William White in "Hart Crane: Bibliographical Addenda," *Bulletin of Bibliography,* XXIV, No. 2 (1963), 35.

B35   Bloomingdale, J. "Three Decades in Periodical Criticism of Hart Crane's 'The Bridge'," *The Papers of the Bibliographical Society of America*, LVII, No. 3 (1963), pp. 364-371.

See also: Bryer, *Fifteen Modern American Authors* (A29), pp. 63-100.

CRANE, STEPHEN

B36   Beebe, Maurice and Thomas A. Gullason. "Criticism of Stephen Crane: A Selected Checklist with an Index to Studies of Separate Works," *Modern Fiction Studies*, V, No. 3 (1959), 282-291.

B37   Hudspeth, Robert N. "A Bibliography of Stephen Crane Scholarship: 1893-1962," *Thoth*, IV, No. 1 (1963), 31-58.

Continued by *Thoth* Annual Bibliography (B39)

B38   Katz, Joseph, comp. *The Merrill Checklist of Stephen Crane*. Columbus, Ohio: Charles E. Merrill, 1969. (*Charles E. Merrill Checklists*)

B39   "The *Thoth* Annual Bibliography of Stephen Crane Scholarship," 1963-

>   Published annually since 1964 in the Spring issue of *Thoth*. Continues Hudspeth (**B37**).

B40   Lettis, Richard, Robert F. McDonnell and William E. Morris, eds. *'The Red Badge of Courage': Text and Criticism.* N.Y.: Harcourt, Brace, 1962, pp. 342-344. (*Harbrace Sourcebooks*)

Cummings, E. E.

B41   Lauter, Paul. *E. E. Cummings: Index to First Lines and Bibliography of Works by and about the Poet.* Denver: Swallow, 1955, pp. 26-44.

De Quincey, Thomas

See: Houtchens, *The English Romantic Poets and Essayists* (A68), pp. 289-332.

Dickens, Charles

B42   Miller, William. *The Dickens Student and Collector: A List of Writings Relating to Charles Dickens and his Works, 1836-1945.* Cambridge, Mass.: Harvard University Pr., 1946.

B43   Ford, George H[arry] and Lauriat Lane, eds. *The Dickens Critics.* Ithaca, N.Y.: Cornell University Pr., 1961, pp. 387-416.

B44   Fielding, K. J. *Charles Dickens: A Critical Introduction.* 2nd ed. rev. and enl. Boston: Houghton Mifflin, 1965, pp. 253-261.

See also: Stevenson, *Victorian Fiction* (A76), pp. 44-53.

Dickinson, Emily

B45   Freis, S. "Emily Dickinson: A Check List of Criticism, 1930-1966," *The Papers of the Bibliographical Society of America*, LXI, No. 10 (1967), 359-385.

B46   Clendenning, Sheila T. *Emily Dickinson: A Bibliography:*

1850-1966. Kent, Ohio: Kent State University Pr., 1968. (*Serif Series*, 3)

DONNE, JOHN

B47   White, William. "John Donne since 1900: A Bibliography of Periodical Articles," *Bulletin of Bibliography,* XVII, No. 5 (1941), 86-89; No. 6, 113; No. 8, 165-171; No. 9, 192-195.

B48   Keynes, Geoffrey [Langdon]. *A Bibliography of Dr. John Donne, Dean of Saint Paul's.* 3rd ed. Cambridge: Cambridge University Pr., 1958.

   Supplement by William White in "Sir Geoffrey Keynes's Bibliography of John Donne: A Review with Addenda," *Bulletin of Bibliography,* XXII, No. 8 (1959), 186-189.

See also: Berry, *A Bibliography of Studies in Metaphysical Poetry* (A56), pp. 25-54.

DOOLITTLE, HILDA

See: H. D.

DOS PASSOS, JOHN

B49   Kallich, Martin. "Bibliography of John Dos Passos," *Bulletin of Bibliography,* XIX, No. 9 (1949), 231-235.

DREISER, THEODORE

B50   Kazin, Alfred and Charles Shapiro, eds. *The Stature of Theodore Dreiser: A Critical Survey of the Man and His Work.* Bloomington: Indiana University Pr., 1955, pp. 271-303.

B51   Atkinson, Hugh C., comp. *The Merrill Checklist of Theodore Dreiser.* Columbus, Ohio: Charles E. Merrill, 1969. (*Charles E. Merrill Checklists*)

See also: Bryer, *Fifteen Modern American Authors* (A29), pp. 101-138.

DRYDEN, JOHN

B52   Monk, Samuel Holt. *John Dryden: A List of Critical Studies Published from 1895 to 1948.* Minneapolis: University of Minnesota Pr., 1950.

Supplemented by W. R. Keast in "Bibliographical Article: Dryden Studies, 1895-1948," *Modern Philology*, XLVIII, No. 3 (1951), 205-210.

B53   Gatto, Louis C. "An Annotated Bibliography of Critical Thought Concerning Dryden's 'Essay of Dramatic Poesy'," *Restoration and 18th Century Theatre Research*, V, No. 1 (1966), 18-29.

ELIOT, GEORGE

B54   Barry, James D. "The Literary Reputation of George Eliot's Fiction: A Supplementary Bibliography," *Bulletin of Bibliography*, XXII, No. 8 (1959), 176-182.

B55   Marshall, William H. "A Selective Bibliography of Writings about George Eliot, to 1965," *Bulletin of Bibliography*, XXV, No. 4 (1967), 88-94.

See also: Stevenson, *Victorian Fiction* (A76), pp. 294-323.

ELIOT, T. S.

B56   Unger, Leonard, ed. *T. S. Eliot: A Selected Critique*. N.Y.: Russell & Russell, 1948, pp. 463-478.

See also: Bryer, *Fifteen Modern American Authors* (A29), pp. 139-174.

EMERSON, RALPH WALDO

B57   Bryer, Jackson R. and Robert A. Rees. *A Checklist of Emerson Criticism, 1951-1961*. Hartford, Conn.: Transcendental Books, 1964.

B58   Sowder, William J. "Emerson's Reviewers and Commentators: Nineteenth-Century Periodical Criticism," *Emerson Society Quarterly*, LIII, No. 4 (1968), 5-51.

Published separately as: Sowder, William J. *Emerson's Reviewers and Commentaries: A Biographical and Bibliographical Analysis of 19th Century Periodical Criticism with a Detailed Index*. Hartford, Conn.: Transcendental Books, 1968.

B59   Ferguson, Alfred R., comp. *The Merrill Checklist of Ralph Waldo Emerson*. Columbus, Ohio: Charles E. Merrill, 1970. (*Charles E. Merrill Checklists*)

B60   "Current Bibliography on Ralph Waldo Emerson," 1958-
      Published in 2-year intervals in the *Emerson Society
      Quarterly.*

See also: Stovall, *Eight American Authors* (A33), pp. 47-99;
      424-428.

FAULKNER, WILLIAM

B61   Vickery, Olga W. and Frederick J[ohn] Hoffman, eds.
      William Faulkner: Three Decades of Criticism. East
      Lansing: Michigan State University Pr., 1960, pp.
      393-428.

B62   Sleeth, Irene Lynn. *William Faulkner: A Bibliography of
      Criticism.* Denver: Swallow, 1962.
      Reprinted from *Twentieth Century Literature*, VIII, No. 1
      (1962), 18-43.

B63   Beebe, Maurice. "Criticism of William Faulkner: A Se-
      lected Checklist," *Modern Fiction Studies*, XIII, No. 1
      (1967), 115-161.

See also: Bryer, *Fifteen Modern American Authors* (A29), pp.
      175-210.

FIELDING, HENRY

B64   Paulson, Ronald, ed. *Fielding: A Collection of Critical
      Essays.* Englewood Cliffs, N.J.: Prentice-Hall, 1962, pp.
      181-186. (*Twentieth Century Views*)

See also: Cordasco, *Eighteenth Century Bibliographies* (A63), pp.
      93-118.

FITZGERALD, EDWARD

See: Ehrsam, *Twelve Victorian Authors* (A73), pp. 78-91.

      Faverty, *The Victorian Poets* (A74), pp. 137-148.

FITZGERALD, F. SCOTT

B65   Beebe, Maurice and Jackson R. Bryer. "Criticism of
      F. Scott Fitzgerald: A Selected Checklist," *Modern
      Fiction Studies*, VII, No. 1 (1961), 82-94.

B66   Bryer, Jackson R. "F. Scott Fitzgerald and his Critics: A Bibliographical Record," *Bulletin of Bibliography*, XXIII, No. 7 (1962), 155-158, 180-183, 201-208.

B67   ―――. *The Critical Reputation of F. Scott Fitzgerald: A Bibliographical Study*. Hamden, Conn.: Archon Books, 1967.

B68   "Checklist," 1957-1969.
> Published quarterly in *Fitzgerald Newsletter*. A corrected and revised version of the original newsletters from No. 1, 1958 to No. 40, 1968 is published in: Bruccoli, Matthew J. *Fitzgerald Newsletter*. Washington, D.C.: NCR Microcard Editions, 1969.

See also: Bryer, *Fifteen Modern American Authors* (A29), pp. 211-238.

FLETCHER, JOHN

See: *Elizabethan Bibliographies Supplements*, No. 8 (B9).

FORD, FORD MADOX

B69   Gerber, Helmut E., ed. "Ford Madox Ford: An Annotated Checklist of Writings about Him," *English Fiction in Transition*, I, No. 2 (1958), 2-19.
> Supplemented by Frank MacShane in "Ford Madox Ford: An Annotated Bibliography of Writings about Him," *English Fiction in Transition*, IV, No. 2 (1961), 19-29.

B70   Harvey, David Dow. *Ford Madox Ford 1873-1939: A Bibliography of Works and Criticism*. Princeton, N.J.: Princeton University Pr., 1962.

B71   Beebe, Maurice and Robert G. Johnson. "Criticism of Ford Madox Ford: A Selected Checklist," *Modern Fiction Studies*, IX, No. 1 (1963), 94-100.

FORSTER, E. M.

B72   Beebe, Maurice and Joseph Brogunier. "Criticism of E. M. Forster: A Selected Checklist," *Modern Fiction Studies*, VII, No. 3 (1961), 284-292.

B73   Bradbury, Malcolm. "Short Guide to Forster Studies," *The Critical Survey*, II, No. 2 (1965), 113-116.

B74   Husain, Syed Hamid. "E. M. Forster," *English Literature in Transition*, IV, No. 2 (1961), 45-53; X, No. 4 (1967), 219-238; XI, No. 11 (1968), 206-216.

FROST, ROBERT

B75   Mertins, [Marshall] Louis and Esther Mertins. *The Intervals of Robert Frost: A Critical Bibliography.* Berkeley and Los Angeles: University of California Pr., 1947.

B76   Parameswaran, Uma. "Robert Frost: A Bibliography of Articles and Books, 1958-1964," *Bulletin of Bibliography* XXV, No. 2 (1967), 46-48; No. 3 (1967), 58, 69, 72.

B77   Grenier, Donald J., comp. *The Merrill Checklist of Robert Frost.* C o l u m b u s, Ohio: Charles E. Merrill, 1969. (*Charles E. Merrill Checklists*)

See also: Bryer, *Fifteen Modern American Authors* (A29), pp. 239-273.

FRY, CHRISTOPHER

B78   Schear, Bernice Larson and Eugene G. Prater. "A Bibliography on Christopher Fry," *Tulane Drama Review*, IV, No. 3 (1960), 88-98.

GALSWORTHY, JOHN

B79   Gerber, Helmut E., ed. "John Galsworthy: An Annotated Checklist of Writings about Him," *English Fiction in Transition*, I, No. 3 (1958), 7-29; VII, No. 2 (1964), 93-110.

GAWAIN POET

See: Pearl Poet.

GISSING, GEORGE

B80   Korg, Jacob. "George Gissing: An Annotated Bibliography of Writings About Him," *English Literature in Transition*, I, No. 1 (1957), 24-28; III, No. 2 (1960), 3-33; VII, No. 1 (1964), 14-26; VII, No. 2 (1964), 73-92.

See also: Stevenson, *Victorian Fiction* (A76), pp. 401-413.

GOLDING, WILLIAM

B81   Baker, James R. *William Golding: A Critical Essay.* N.Y.: St. Martin's Pr., 1965, pp. 97-102.

B82   Nelson, [Francis] William. *William Golding's 'Lord of the Flies': A Source Book.* N.Y.: Odyssey Pr., 1963.

        An anthology of articles and a useful selection of related readings, including excerpts from Freud, Frazer, Jung, and others.

GOWER, JOHN

See: Fisher, *The Medieval Literature of Western Europe* (A45), p. 123.

GRAY, THOMAS

B83   Northup, Clark Sutherland. *A Bibliography of Thomas Gray.* New Haven, Conn.: Yale University Pr., 1917.

B84   Starr, Herbert W. *A Bibliography of Thomas Gray. With material Supplementary to C. S. Northup's 'Bibliography of Thomas Gray'.* Philadelphia: University of Pennsylvania Pr. for Temple University Publications, 1953.

GREENE, GRAHAM

B85   Birmingham, William. "Graham Greene Criticism: A Bibliographical Study," *Thought,* XXVII, No. 104 (1952), 72-100.

B86   Beebe, Maurice, "Criticism of Graham Greene: A Selected Checklist with an Index to Studies of Separate Works," *Modern Fiction Studies,* III, No. 3 (1957), 281-288.

B87   Evans, Robert O[wen], ed. *Graham Greene: Some Critical Considerations.* Lexington: University of Kentucky Pr., 1963, pp. 245-276.

H. D.

B88   Bryer, Jackson R. and Pamela Roblyer. "H. D.: A Preliminary Checklist," *Contemporary Literature,* X, No. 4 (1969), 632-675.

HARDY, THOMAS

B89   Beebe, Maurice, Bonnie Culotta and Erin Marcus. "Criticism of Thomas Hardy: A Selected Checklist," *Modern Fiction Studies*, VI, No. 3 (1960), 258-279.

B90   Weber, Carl J[efferson], comp. *The First Hundred Years of Thomas Hardy 1840-1940: A Centenary Bibliography of Hardiana.* N.Y.: Russell & Russell, 1965.

See also: Ehrsam, *Twelve Victorian Authors* (A73), pp. 92-125.

Faverty, *The Victorian Poets* (A74), pp. 367-375.

Stevenson, *Victorian Fiction* (A76), pp. 349-387.

HAWTHORNE, NATHANIEL

B91   Jones, Buford. *A Checklist of Hawthorne Criticism: 1951-1966.* Hartford, Conn.: Transcendental Books, 1967.

B92   Clark, C. E. Frazer, comp. *The Merrill Checklist of Nathaniel Hawthorne.* Columbus, Ohio: Charles E. Merrill, 1970. (*Charles E. Merrill Checklists*)

B93   Phillips, Robert S. " 'The Scarlet Letter': A Selected Checklist of Criticism," *Bulletin of Bibliography*, XXIII, No. 9 (1962), 213-216.

See also: Stovall, *Eight American Authors* (A33), pp. 100-133; 428-434.

HAZLITT, WILLIAM

See: Houtchens, *The English Romantic Poets and Essayists* (A68), pp. 75-114.

HEMINGWAY, ERNEST

B94   Hanneman, Audre. *Ernest Hemingway: A Comprehensive Bibliography.* Princeton, N.J.: Princeton University Pr., 1967.

> Includes books, newspaper and periodical articles, and reviews, from 1918-1965.

B95   Beebe, Maurice and John Feaster. "Criticism of Ernest Hemingway: A Selected Checklist," *Modern Fiction Studies*, XIV, No. 3 (1968), 337-369.

B96   White, William, comp. *The Merrill Checklist of Ernest Hemingway*. Columbus, Ohio: Charles E. Merrill, 1970. (*Charles E. Merrill Checklists*)

See also: Brycr, *Fifteen Modern American Authors* (A29), pp. 275-300.

HERBERT, GEORGE

B97   Tannenbaum, Samuel A[aron] and Dorothy R. Tannenbaum. *George Herbert: A Concise Bibliography*. N.Y.: Samuel A. Tannenbaum, 1946. (*Elizabethan Bibliographies*, 35)

See also: Berry, *A Bibliography of Studies in Metaphysical Poetry* (A56), pp. 57-64.

HERRICK, ROBERT

See: *Elizabethan Bibliographies Supplements*, 3 (B113).

HOPKINS, GERARD MANLEY

B98   Patricia, Sister Mary. "Forty Years of Criticism: A Chronological Check List of Criticism of the Works of Gerard Manley Hopkins from 1909 to 1949," *Bulletin of Bibliography*, XX, No. 2 (1950), 38-44; No. 3, 63-67.

B99   Charney, Maurice. "A Bibliographical Study of Hopkins Criticism, 1918-1949," *Thought*, XXV, No. 97 (1950), 297-326.

B100   Cohen, Edward H. *Works and Criticism of Gerard Manley Hopkins: A Comprehensive Bibliography*. Washington, D.C.: Catholic University of America Pr., 1969.

B101   Seelhammer, Ruth. *Hopkins Collected at Gonzaga*. Chicago: Loyola University Pr., 1970.

See also: Faverty, *The Victorian Poets* (A74), pp. 318-351.

HOUSMAN, A. E.

B102   Ehrsam, Theodore G[eorge], comp. *A Bibliography of Alfred Edward Housman.* Boston: Faxon, 1941. (*Useful Reference Series,* 66)

B103   Stallman, Robert Wooster. "Annotated Bibliography of A. E. Housman: A Critical Study," *PMLA,* LX, No. 2 (1945), 463-502.

See also: Faverty, *The Victorian Poets* (A74), pp. 391-397.

HUNT, LEIGH

See: Bernbaum, "Keats, Shelley, Byron and Hunt. A Critical Sketch of Important Books and Articles Concerning them Published in 1940-1950," *Keats-Shelley Journal* (B179), pp. 73-85.

Houtchens, *The English Romantic Poets and Essayists* (A68), pp. 255-288.

HUXLEY, ALDOUS

B104   Eschelbach, Claire John and Joyce Lee Shober. *Aldous Huxley: A Bibliography, 1916-1959.* Berkeley and Los Angeles: University of California Pr., 1961.

JAMES, HENRY

B105   Beebe, Maurice and William T. Stafford. "Criticism of Henry James: A Selected Checklist," *Modern Fiction Studies,* XII, No. 1 (1966), 117-178.
        Largely supersedes the checklist in *Modern Fiction Studies,* III, No. 1 (1957), 73-96.

B106   Willen, Gerald, ed. *A Casebook on Henry James's 'The Turn of the Screw'.* N.Y.: Crowell, 1960, pp. 319-322.

See also: Stovall, *Eight American Authors* (A33), pp. 364-418; 458-468.

JOHNSON, SAMUEL

B107   Clifford, James L[owry]. *Johnsonian Studies: 1887-1950:*

A Survey and Bibliography. Minneapolis: University of Minnesota Pr., 1951.

Continued by Wahba (B108).

B108 Wahba, Magdi, ed. *Johnsonian Studies: Including a Bibliography of Johnsonian Studies, 1950-1960.* Compiled by James L. Clifford and Donald J. Greene. Cairo: Société Orientale de Publicité, 1962.

Continues Clifford (B107).

JONSON, BEN

B109 Tannenbaum, Samuel A[aron]. *Ben Jonson (A Concise Bibliography).* N.Y.: Scholars' Facsimiles and Reprints, 1938. (*Elizabethan Bibliographies*, 2)

Supplement by Samuel A. Tannenbaum and Dorothy R. Tannenbaum, *Supplement to Ben Jonson, A Concise Bibliography.* N.Y.: Samuel A. Tannenbaum, 1947.

B110 Steensma, Robert C. "Ben Jonson: A Checklist of Editions, Biography, and Criticism, 1947-1964," *Research Opportunities in Renaissance Drama,* IX (1966), 29-46.

B111 Guffey, George Robert, comp. *Robert Herrick, 1949-1965; Ben Jonson, 1947-1965; Thomas Randolph, 1949-1965.* London: Nether Pr., 1968. (*Elizabethan Bibliographies Supplements,* 3)

JOYCE, JAMES

B112 Beebe, Maurice and Walton Litz. "Criticism of James Joyce: A Selected Checklist with an Index to Studies of Separate Works," *Modern Fiction Studies,* IV, No. 1 (1958), 71-99.

B113 Deming, Robert H. *A Bibliography of James Joyce Studies.* Lawrence: University of Kansas Libraries, 1964. (*Library Series,* 18)

B114 Beebe, Maurice, Phillip F. Herring and Walton Litz. "Criticism of James Joyce: A Selected Checklist," *Modern Fiction Studies,* XV, No. 1 (1969), 105-182.

B115   "Supplemental James Joyce Checklist," 1959-
　　　　Published annually since 1965 in *James Joyce Quarterly*.

B116   Morris, William E. and Clifford A. Nault, Jr. "A One
　　　　Hundred Item Checklist of Publications Relevant to the
　　　　'Portrait'," in their *Portraits of an Artist: A Casebook on
　　　　James Joyce's 'A Portrait of The Artist as a Young Man'*.
　　　　N.Y.: Odyssey Pr., 1962, pp. 293-298.

KEATS, JOHN

B117   MacGillivray, J[ames] R[obertson]. *Keats: A Bibliography
　　　　and Reference Guide, with an Essay on Keats' Repu-
　　　　tation*. Toronto: University of Toronto Pr., 1949. (*Uni-
　　　　versity of Toronto. Dept. of English. Studies and Texts,* 3)

B118   Rice, Sister Pio Maria. "A Classified Bibliography of Critical
　　　　Writings on John Keats' Poems Occurring in Periodicals
　　　　over the Fifteen Year Period, 1947-1961," *Bulletin of
　　　　Bibliography*, XXIV, No. 7 (1965), 167-168; No. 8,
　　　　187-192.

See also: Bernbaum, "Keats, Shelley, Byron and Hunt. A Critical
　　　　Sketch of Important Books and Articles Concerning them
　　　　Published in 1940-1950," *Keats-Shelley Journal* (B179),
　　　　pp. 73-85.

　　　　Raysor, *The English Romantic Poets* (A69), pp. 233-307.

KIPLING, RUDYARD

B119   Gerber, Helmut E. and Edward Lauterbach, comps. "Rud-
　　　　yard Kipling: An Annotated Bibliography of Writings
　　　　about Him," *English Fiction in Transition,* III, Nos. 3-5
　　　　(1960), 1-235.

See also: Ehrsam, *Twelve Victorian Authors* (A73), pp. 128-161.

LAMB, CHARLES

See: Houtchens, *The English Romantic Poets and Essayists*
　　　　(A68), pp. 37-74.

LANDOR, WALTER SAVAGE

See: Houtchens, *The English Romantic Poets and Essayists* (A68), pp. 221-254.

LANGLAND, WILLIAM

B120 Bloomfield, Morton W. "Present State of 'Piers Plowman' Studies," *Speculum*, XIV, No. 2 (1939), 215-232.

A review of *Piers Plowman* scholarship up to 1939.

See also: Fisher, *The Medieval Literature of Western Europe* (A45), pp. 106-110.

LAWRENCE, D. H.

B121 White, William. *D. H. Lawrence: A Checklist, 1931-1950*. Detroit, Mich.: Wayne University Pr., 1950.

B122 Beebe, Maurice and Anthony Tommassi. "Criticism of D. H. Lawrence: A Selected Checklist of Criticism with an Index to Studies of Separate Works," *Modern Fiction Studies*, V, No. 1 (1959), 83-98.

Continued by Richard D. Beards and G. B. Crump, in "D. H. Lawrence: Ten Years of Criticism: 1959-1968, A Checklist," *D. H. Lawrence Review*, I, No. 3 (1968), 245-285.

B123 "D. H. Lawrence: Criticism," Sept. 1968-

Published annually since 1970 in the Spring issue of *D. H. Lawrence Review*.

LEWIS, SINCLAIR

B124 Moscow, Vsesoyuznaia Gosudarstvennaya Biblioteka Inostrannoy Literatury. *Sinkler L'iuis*. Moscow, 1939.

English criticism included.

B125 Dooley, D[avid] J[oseph]. *The Art of Sinclair Lewis*. Lincoln: University of Nebraska Pr., 1967, pp. 269-277.

LOWRY, MALCOLM

B126 Birney, Earle and Margerie Lowry. "Malcolm Lowry (1909-1957): A Bibliography. Part II: Works about Malcolm

Lowry," *Canadian Literature*, VIII (1961), 80-84 and XI (1962), 90-95.

MACLENNAN, HUGH

B127   Goetsch, Paul. *Das Romanwerk Hugh MacLennans: Eine Studie zum literarischen Nationalismus in Kanada.* Hamburg: Gruyter, 1961, pp. 129-139.

MALAMUD, BERNARD

B128   Kosofsky, Rita Nathalie. *Bernard Malamud: An Annotated Checklist.* Kent, Ohio: Kent State University Pr., 1969. (*Serif Series,* 7)

MALORY, SIR THOMAS

See: Fisher, *The Medieval Literature of Western Europe* (A45), pp. 98-101.

MANSFIELD, KATHERINE

B129   Mantz, Ruth Elvish. *The Critical Bibliography of Katherine Mansfield.* London: Constable, 1931.

MARLOWE, CHRISTOPHER

B130   Johnson, Robert C., comp. *Christopher Marlowe, 1946-1965.* London: Nether Pr., 1967. (*Elizabethan Bibliographies Supplements,* 6)

MARVELL, ANDREW

B131   Toliver, Harold E. *Marvell's Ironic Vision.* New Haven, Conn.: Yale University Pr., 1965, pp. 214-226.

B132   Donovan, Dennis G., comp. *Andrew Marvell, 1927-1967.* London: Nether Pr., 1969. (*Elizabethan Bibliographies Supplements,* 12)

See also: Berry, *A Bibliography of Studies in Metaphysical Poetry* (A56), pp. 67-76.

MAUGHAM, SOMERSET

B133   Jonas, Klaus W. *A Bibliography of the Writings of Somerset*

Maugham. Ann Arbor, Mich.: Edwards Bros., 1950.

Supplement by Klaus W. Jonas in "More Maughamiana," *The Papers of the Bibliographical Society of America,* XLIV, No. 4 (1950), 378-383.

MELVILLE, HERMAN

B134 Stern, Milton R. *The Fine Hammered Steel of Herman Melville: With a Checklist of Melville Studies.* Urbana: University of Illinois Pr., 1957, pp. 251-291.

B135 *Melville Bibliography, 1952-1957.* Providence, R. I.: Melville Society, 1959.

B136 Beebe, Maurice, Harrison Hayford and Gordon Roper. "Criticism of Herman Melville: A Selected Checklist," *Modern Fiction Studies,* VIII, No. 3 (1962), 312-346.

B137 Zimmerman, Michael. "Herman Melville in the 1920's: An Annotated Bibliography," *Bulletin of Bibliography,* XXIV, No. 5 (1964), 117-120 and XXIV, No. 6 (1965), 139-144.

B138 Vann, J. Don. "A Selected Checklist of Melville Criticism, 1958-1968," *Studies in the Novel,* I, No. 4 (1969), 507-535.

See also: Stovall, *Eight American Authors* (A33), pp. 207-270; 438-445.

MEREDITH, GEORGE

B139 Forman, Maurice Buxton. *A Bibliography of the Writings in Prose and Verse of George Meredith.* Edinburgh: Bibliographical Society, 1922.
Supplement, 1924.

Secondary material listed in the supplement volume.

B140 Sawin, Lewis H. "George Meredith: A Bibliography of Meredithiana, 1920-1953," *Bulletin of Bibliography,* XXI, No. 8 (1955), 186-191; No. 9 (1956), 215-216.

See also: Stevenson, *Victorian Fiction* (A76), pp. 324-348.

MILL, JOHN STUART

B141   Hascall, Dudley L. and John M. Robson. "Bibliography of Writings on Mill," *The Mill News Letter*, I, No. I-V, No. 2 (1965-1970).

MILLAY, EDNA ST. VINCENT

B142   Brenni, Vito J. and John E. James. "Edna St. Vincent Millay: Selected Criticism," *Bulletin of Bibliography*, XXIII, No. 8 (1962), 177-178.

MILLER, ARTHUR

B143   Eissenstat, Martha Turnquist. "Arthur Miller: A Bibliography," *Modern Drama*, V, No. 1 (1962), 93-106.

B144   Hayashi, Tetsumaro. *Arthur Miller Criticism (1930-1967)*. Metuchen, N.J.: Scarecrow Pr., 1969.

MILLER, HENRY

B145   Renken, Maxine. "Bibliography of Henry Miller: 1945-1961: Part III," *Twentieth Century Literature*, VII, No. 1 (1962), 186-190.

MILTON, JOHN

B146   Stevens, David Harrison. *Reference Guide to Milton: From 1800 to the Present Day.* Chicago: University of Chicago Pr., 1930.

> Supplemented by Francis H. Fletcher in "Contributions to a Milton Bibliography, 1800-1930, being a list of Addenda to Stevens's 'Reference Guide to Milton'," *University of Illinois Studies in Language and Literature*, XVI, No. 1 (1931), 7-166.

B147   Hanford, James Holly, comp. *Milton.* N.Y.: Appleton-Century-Crofts, 1966. (*Goldentree Bibliographies*)

B148   Huckabay, Calvin, comp. *John Milton: An Annotated Bibliography 1929-1968.* Rev. ed. Pittsburgh, Pa.: Duquesne University Pr., 1969. (*Duquesne Studies, Philological Series*)

B149   "Abstracts," 1967-

A quarterly listing since 1968 of articles with brief abstracts in *Milton Quarterly* (formerly *Milton Newsletter*).

B150   Stratman, Carl J. "Checklist of Criticism of 'Samson Agonistes'," *Restoration and 18th Century Theatre Research*, IV, No. 2 (1965), 2-10.

MOORE, GEORGE

B151   Gerber, Helmut E. "George Moore: An Annotated Bibliography of Writings About Him," *English Fiction in Transition*, II, No. 2 (1959), 1-91; III, No. 2 (1960), 34-46; IV, No. 2 (1961), 30-42.

See also: Stevenson, *Victorian Fiction* (A76), pp. 388-401.

MOORE, MARIANNE

B152   Sheehy, Eugene P[aul] and Kenneth A. Lohf, comps. *The Achievement of Marianne Moore: A Bibliography, 1907-1957*. N.Y.: New York Public Library, 1958.

MORRIS, WILLIAM

B153   "William Morris and his Circle: A Selective Bibliography of Publications," 1960-

Published irregularly in *The Journal of the William Morris Society* since summer, 1964, by W. E. Fredeman.

See also: Ehrsam, *Twelve Victorian Authors* (A73), pp. 162-187.

Faverty, *The Victorian Poets* (A74), pp. 293-307.

Fredeman, *Pre-Raphaelitism* (A75), pp. 162-175.

MURDOCH, IRIS

B154   Widmann, R. L. "An Iris Murdoch Checklist," *Critique*, X, No. 1 (1967), 17-29.

B155   Culley, Anne and John Feaster. "Criticism of Iris Murdoch: A Selected Checklist," *Modern Fiction Studies*, XV, No. 3 (1969), 449-457.

NABOKOV, VLADIMIR

B156   Bryer, Jackson R. and Thomas H. Bergin. "A Checklist of
        Nabokov Criticism in English," *Wisconsin Studies in
        Contemporary Literature*, VIII, No. 2 (1967), 318-364.

> Also published in: Dembo, L[awrence] S[anford], ed.
> *Nabokov, the Man and his Work*. Madison: University of
> Wisconsin Pr., 1967.

O'CASEY, SEAN

B157   Carpenter, Charles A. "Sean O'Casey Studies through
        1964," *Modern Drama*, X, No. 1 (1967), 17-23.

O'NEILL, EUGENE

B158   Bryer, Jackson R. "Forty Years of O'Neill Criticism: A
        Selected Bibliography," *Modern Drama*, IV, No. 2
        (1961), 196-216.

B159   Cargill, Oscar [and others], eds. *O'Neill and his Plays: Four
        Decades of Criticism*. N.Y.: New York University Pr.,
        1961, pp. 487-517.

B160   Miller, Jordan Y[ale]. *Eugene O'Neill and the American
        Critic: A Summary and Bibliographical Checklist*. Hamden,
        Conn.: Shoestring Pr., 1962, pp. 175-465.

See also: Bryer, *Fifteen Modern American Authors* (A29), pp.
        301-322.

ORWELL, GEORGE

B161   Zeke, Zoltan G. and William White. "George Orwell: A
        Selected Bibliography," *Bulletin of Bibliography*, XXIII,
        No. 5 (1961), 110-114; No. 6, 140-144; No. 7 (1962),
        166-168; No. 10 (1963), 224-230; XXIV, No. 1 (1963),
        19-24; No. 2, 36-40; No. 8 (1965), 180-186.

PEARL, POET

See: Fisher, *The Medieval Literature of Western Europe* (A45),
        pp. 91-93.

PINTER, HAROLD

B162 Gordon, L. G. "Pigeonholing Pinter: A Bibliography," *Theatre Documentation*, I, No. 1 (1968), 3-20.

POE, EDGAR ALLAN

B163 Robins, J[ohn] Albert, comp. *The Merrill Checklist of Edgar Allan Poe*. Columbus, Ohio: Charles E. Merrill, 1969. (*Charles E. Merrill Checklists*)

B164 "Current Poe Studies," 1967-
> Published semi-annually since April, 1968, in *Poe Newsletter*. There is also an annotated bibliography published annually in the Fall issue.

See also: Stovall, *Eight American Authors* (A33), pp. 1-46.

POPE, ALEXANDER

B165 Tobin, James Edward. *Alexander Pope: A List of Critical Studies Published from 1895 to 1944*. N.Y.: Cosmopolitan Science and Art Service Co., 1945.

PORTER, KATHERINE ANNE

B166 Waldrip, Louise and Shirley Ann Baker. *A Bibliography of the Works of Katherine Anne Porter and a Bibliography of the Criticism of the Works of Katherine Anne Porter*. Metuchen, N.J.: Scarecrow Pr., 1969.

POUND, EZRA

B167 "Bibliography," 1909-1956.
> A bibliography and a "Works in Progress" section published in each issue of *The Pound Newsletter* from Jan., 1954-April, 1956.

See also: Bryer, *Fifteen Modern American Authors* (A29), pp. 323-344.

RICHARDSON, SAMUEL

See: Cordasco, *Eighteenth Century Bibliographies* (A63), pp. 55-72.

ROBINSON, EDWIN ARLINGTON

B168   Anderson, Wallace L[udwig]. *Edwin Arlington Robinson: A Critical Introduction.* Boston: Houghton, Mifflin, 1967, pp. 155-165.

See also: Bryer, *Fifteen Modern American Authors* (A29), pp. 345-367.

ROSSETTI, CHRISTINA

See: Ehrsam, *Twelve Victorian Authors* (A73), pp. 190-199.

Faverty, *The Victorian Poets* (A74), pp. 284-293.

Fredeman, *Pre-Raphaelitism* (A75), pp. 176-182.

ROSSETTI, DANTE GABRIEL

See: Ehrsam, *Twelve Victorian Authors* (A73), pp. 202-225.

Faverty, *The Victorian Poets* (A74), pp. 262-284.

Fredeman, *Pre-Raphaelitism* (A75), pp. 90-132.

RUSKIN, JOHN

See: Fredeman, *Pre-Raphaelitism* (A75), pp. 183-185.

SALINGER, J. D.

B169   Fiene, Donald M. "J. D. Salinger: A Bibliography: Part II," *Wisconsin Studies in Contemporary Literature*, IV, No. 1 (1963), 117-149.

> Supplemented by David D. Galloway. "A J. D. Salinger Checklist," in his *The Absurd Hero in American Fiction: Updike, Styron, Bellow, Salinger.* Austin: University of Texas Pr., 1966, pp. 226-251.

B170   Beebe, Maurice and Jennifer Sperry. "Criticism of J. D. Salinger: A Selected Checklist," *Modern Fiction Studies*, XII, No. 3 (1966), 377-390.

B171   Lettis, Richard. *J. D. Salinger: 'The Catcher in the Rye'.* Great Neck, N.Y.: Barron's Educational Series, 1964, pp. 44-50. (*Barron's Studies in American Literature*)

SCOTT, SIR WALTER

See: Houtchens, *The English Romantic Poets and Essayists* (A68), pp. 115-154.

SHAKESPEARE, WILLIAM

B172   Smith, Gordon Ross. *A Classified Shakespeare Bibliography, 1936-1958.* University Park: Pennsylvania State University Pr., 1963.

B173   Berman, Ronald. *A Reader's Guide to Shakespeare's Plays: A Discursive Bibliography.* Chicago: Scott, Foresman & Co., 1965.

B174   "Annual Bibliography," 1924-1949.
        Published in *Shakespeare Association of America Bulletin.* Continued by B175.

B175   "Shakespeare: An Annotated Bibliography," 1950-
        Published annually since 1950 in the Spring issue of *Shakespeare Quarterly.* Lists bibliographies, surveys, collections, editions, translations, books, and articles about Shakespeare. Continues B174.

SHAW, GEORGE BERNARD

B176   Farley, Earl and Marvin Carlson. "A Selected Bibliography (1945-1955) Part I: Books, Part II: Periodicals," *Modern Drama*, II, No. 2 (1959), 188-202; No. 3 (1959), 295-323.

B177   Keough, Lawrence C. "George Bernard Shaw, 1946-1955: A Selected Bibliography," *Bulletin of Bibliography*, XXII, No. 10 (1959), 224-226; XXIII, No. 1 (1960), 20-24; No. 2 (1960), 36-41.

B178   "A Continuing Checklist of Shaviana," 1950-
        Published in each issue of *The Shaw Review* since 1951.

SHELLEY, PERCY BYSSHE

B179   Bernbaum, Ernest. "Keats, Shelley, Byron, and Hunt. A Critical Sketch of Important Books and Articles Concerning them Published in 1940-1950," *Keats-Shelley Journal*, I (1952), 73-85.

Continued by the current bibliography in *Keats-Shelley Journal* (A70)

B180   Cameron, Kenneth Neill. "Shelley Scholarship, 1940-1953: A Critical Survey," *Keats-Shelley Journal,* III (1954), 89-109.

See also: Raysor, *The English Romantic Poets* (A69), pp. 184-232.

SIDNEY, SIR PHILIP

B181   Tannenbaum, Samuel A[aron]. *Sir Philip Sidney (A Concise Bibliography).* N.Y.: Tannenbaum, 1941. (*Elizabethan Bibliographies,* 23)

B182   Guffey, George Robert, comp. *Samuel Daniel, 1942-1965; Michael Drayton, 1941-1965; Sir Philip Sidney, 1941-1965.* London: Nether Pr., 1967. (*Elizabethan Bibliographies Supplements,* 7)

SMOLLETT, TOBIAS

B183   Korte, Donald M. *An Annotated Bibliography of Smollett Scholarship, 1946-1968.* Toronto: University of Toronto Pr., 1969.

See also: Cordasco, *Eighteenth Century Bibliographies* (A63), pp. 7-53, 207-230.
Supplements Cordasco, *Eighteenth Century Bibliographies* (A63)

SOUTHEY, ROBERT

See: Houtchens, *The English Romantic Poets and Essayists* (A68), pp. 155-182.

SPENSER, EDMUND

B184   Carpenter, Frederic Ives. *A Reference Guide to Edmund Spenser.* Chicago: University of Chicago Pr., 1923.

B185   Atkinson, Dorothy F. *Edmund Spenser: A Bibliographical Supplement.* Baltimore: Johns Hopkins Pr., 1937.
Continued by McNeir (B186).

B186   McNeir, Waldo F. and Foster Provost. *Annotated Bibliography of Edmund Spenser, 1937-1960.* Pittsburgh, Pa.:

Duquesne University Pr., 1962. (*Duquesne Studies, Philological Series*, 3)
Continues Atkinson (B185).

STEIN, GERTRUDE

B187 Sawyer, Julian. *Gertrude Stein: A Bibliography*. N.Y.: Arrow Editions, 1940.

B188 ———. "Gertrude Stein: A Checklist Comprising Critical and Miscellaneous Writings About Her Work, Life, and Personality from 1913-1943," *Bulletin of Bibliography*, XVII, No. 10 (1943), 211-212; XVIII, No. 1 (1943), 11-13.

STEINBECK, JOHN

B189 Steele, Joan. "John Steinbeck: A Checklist of Biographical, Critical, and Bibliographical Material," *Bulletin of Bibliography*, XXIV, No. 7 (1965), 149-152, 162-163.

B190 Beebe, Maurice and Jackson R. Bryer. "Criticism of John Steinbeck: A Selected Checklist," *Modern Fiction Studies*, XI, No. 1 (1965), 90-103.

B191 Hayashi, Tetsumaro, comp. *John Steinbeck: A Concise Bibliography (1930-1965)*. Metuchen, N.J.: Scarecrow Pr., 1967.

B192 Donahue, Agnes McNeill, comp. *A Casebook on 'The Grapes of Wrath'*. N.Y.: Crowell, 1968. (*Crowell Literary Casebooks*)

See also: Bryer, *Fifteen Modern American Authors* (A29), pp. 369-387.

STERNE, LAWRENCE

B193 Hartley, Lodwick [Charles]. *Lawrence Sterne in the Twentieth Century: An Essay and a Bibliography of Sternean Studies, 1900-1965*. Chapel Hill: University of North Carolina Pr., 1966, pp. 75-180.

See also: Cordasco, *Eighteenth Century Bibliographies* (A63), pp. 73-92.

STEVENS, WALLACE

B194   Brown, Ashley and Robert S. Haller, eds. *The Achievement of Wallace Stevens.* Philadelphia, Pa.: Lippincott, 1962, pp. 271-287.

> Supplemented by R. S. Mitchell in *Bulletin of Bibliography*, XXIII, No. 9 (1962), 208-211; No. 10 (1963), 232-233.

B195   Morse, Samuel French, Jackson R. Bryer, and Joseph N. Riddell. *Wallace Stevens Checklist and Bibliography of Stevens Criticism.* Denver: Swallow, 1963.

B196   Huguelet, T[heodore] L. *The Merrill Checklist of Wallace Stevens.* Columbus, Ohio: Charles E. Merrill Pub. Co., 1970. (*Charles E. Merrill Checklists*)

See also: Bryer, *Fifteen Modern American Authors* (A29), pp. 389-423.

SWIFT, JONATHAN

B197   Landa, Louis A. and James Edward Tobin. *Jonathan Swift: A List of Critical Studies Published from 1895 to 1945.* N.Y.: Cosmopolitan Science and Art Service Co., 1945. (*Eighteenth Century Bibliographical Pamphlets*)

> Continued by Stathis (B199).

B198   Teerink, Herman. *A Bibliography of the Writings of Jonathan Swift.* 2nd ed., rev. and corr., ed. Arthur H. Scouten. Philadelphia: University of Pennsylvania Pr., 1963.

B199   Stathis, James [J.], comp. *Bibliography of Swift Studies, 1945-1965.* Nashville, Tenn.: Vanderbilt University Pr., 1967.

> Continues Landa (B197).

SWINBURNE, A. C.

See: Ehrsam, *Twelve Victorian Authors* (A73), pp. 264-299.

Faverty, *The Victorian Poets* (A74), pp. 227-250.

Fredeman, *Pre-Raphaelitism* (A75), pp. 216-220.

TENNYSON, ALFRED

B200   Hunt, John Dixon. "A Short Guide to Tennyson Studies," *The Critical Survey*, II, No. 3 (1965), 163-168.

B201   Tennyson, Charles and Christine Fall. *Alfred Tennyson: An Annotated Bibliography*. Athens: University of Georgia Pr., 1967.

See also: Ehrsam, *Twelve Victorian Authors* (A73), pp. 300-362.

Faverty, *The Victorian Poets* (A74), pp. 34-80.

THACKERAY, WILLIAM MAKEPEACE

B202   Flamm, Dudley. *Thackeray's Critics: An Annotated Bibliography of British and American Criticism 1836-1901*. Chapel Hill: University of North Carolina Pr., 1966.

See also: Stevenson, *Victorian Fiction* (A76), pp. 154-187.

THOMAS, DYLAN

B203   Brinnin, John Malcolm, ed. *A Casebook on Dylan Thomas*. N.Y.: Crowell, 1960, pp. 295-310. (*Crowell Literary Casebooks*)

B204   Theisen, Sister Lois. "Dylan Thomas: Secondary Criticism," *Bulletin of Bibliography*, XXVI, No. 2 (1969), 36, 59-60.

THOREAU, HENRY DAVID

B205   White, William. "A Henry David Thoreau Bibliography, 1908-1937," *Bulletin of Bibliography*, XVI, No. 5 (1938), 90-92; No. 6, 111-113; No. 8 (1939), 163; No. 9, 181-182; No. 10, 199-202.
   Continued by *Thoreau Society Bulletin* bibliography (B207).

B206   Hildenbrand, Christopher A. *Bibliography of Scholarship about Henry David Thoreau: 1940-1967*. Hays: Fort Hays Kansas State College, 1967. (*Fort Hays Studies— New Series, Bibliography Series*, 3)

B207   "Additions to the Thoreau Bibliography," 1940-

Published in each issue of the *Thoreau Society Bulletin* since 1941. Continues White (B205).

See also: Stovall, *Eight American Authors* (A33), pp. 153-206, 434-438.

TROLLOPE, ANTHONY

B208 Irwin, Mary Leslie. *Anthony Trollope: A Bibliography.* N.Y.: Burt Franklin, 1968. (*Burt Franklin: Bibliography and Reference Series*, 180)

See also: Stevenson, *Victorian Fiction* (A76), pp. 188-213.

TWAIN, MARK

B209 Asselineau, Roger. *Literary Reputation of Mark Twain from 1910 to 1950: A Critical Essay and a Bibliography.* Paris: Marcel Didier, 1954, pp. 67-226.

B210 Wagenknecht, Edward [Charles]. *Mark Twain: The Man and his Work: Third Edition With a Commentary on Mark Twain Criticism and Scholarship since 1960.* Norman: University of Oklahoma Pr., 1967, pp. 247-264.

B211 Beebe, Maurice and John Feaster. "Criticism of Mark Twain: A Selected Checklist," *Modern Fiction Studies,* XIV, No. 1 (1968), 93-139.

See also: Stovall, *Eight American Authors* (A33), pp. 319-363.

UPDIKE, JOHN

B212 Taylor, Charles Clarke. *John Updike: A Bibliography.* Kent, Ohio: Kent State University Pr., 1969. (*Serif Series*, 4)

WAUGH, EVELYN

B213 Doyle, Paul A. "Evelyn Waugh: A Selected Bibliography (1926-1956)," *Bulletin of Bibliography*, XXII, No. 3 (1957), 57-62.

B214 Kosok, Heinz. "Evelyn Waugh: A Checklist of Criticism," *Twentieth Century Literature*, XI, No. 4 (1966), 211-215.

B215 "The Year's Work in Waugh Studies," 1966-

Published annually since 1967 in the April issue of *Evelyn Waugh Newsletter*. Current checklists and bibliographies also appear in the Spring and Winter issues.

WELLS, H. G.

B216 Raknem, Ingvald, *H. G. Wells and his Critics*. Oslo: Universitetsforlaget, 1962, pp. 446-475.

WHITMAN, WALT

B217 Allen, Gay Wilson. *Twenty-five Years of Walt Whitman Bibliography, 1918-1942*. Boston: Faxon, 1943. (*Bulletin of Bibliography Pamphlets,* 88)

Reprinted from: *Bulletin of Bibliography*, XV, No. 5 (1934), 84-88; XVII, No. 10 (1943), 209-210; XVIII, No. 1 (1943), 9-10.
Supplemented by: Allen, Gay Wilson and Evie Allison Wilson. "Walt Whitman Bibliography, 1944-1954," *Walt Whitman Foundation Bulletin*, VIII (April, 1955), 10-34.

B218 Tanner, [James] T. F. *Walt Whitman: A Supplementary Bibliography: 1961-1967*. Kent, Ohio: Kent State University Pr., 1969. (*Serif Series*, 5)

B219 "Whitman: A Current Bibliography," 1954-

Bibliography by William White published quarterly in the *Walt Whitman Review* since 1955.

See also: Stovall, *Eight American Authors* (A33), pp. 271-318, 445-451.

WILDER, THORNTON

B220 Kosok, Heinz. "Thornton Wilder: A Bibliography of Criticism," *Twentieth Century Literature*, IX, No. 2 (1963), 93-100.

WILLIAMS, TENNESSEE

B221   Dony, Nadine. "Tennessee Williams: A Selected Bibliography," *Modern Drama,* I, No. 3 (1958), 181-191; II, No. 3 (1959), 220-223.

WILLIAMS, WILLIAM CARLOS

B222   Wagner, Linda Welshimer. "A Decade of Discovery, 1953-1963: Checklist of Criticism, William Carlos Williams' Poetry," *Twentieth Century Literature,* X, No. 4 (1965), 166-169.

B223   Durst, Martin I. "William Carlos Williams: A Bibliography," *West Coast Review,* I, No. 2 (1966), 49-54; No. 3 (1967), 44-49.

WOLFE, THOMAS

B224   Johnson, Elmer D. *Of Time and Thomas Wolfe: A Bibliography with a Character Index of His Works.* N.Y.: Scarecrow Pr., 1959.

B225   Beebe, Maurice and Leslie A. Field. "Criticism of Thomas Wolfe: A Selected Checklist," *Modern Fiction Studies,* XI, No. 3 (1965), 315-328.

   Also published in: Field, Leslie A., ed. *Thomas Wolfe: Three Decades of Criticism.* N.Y.: New York University Pr., 1968, pp. 273-293.

B226   Johnson, Elmer D. *Thomas Wolfe: A Checklist.* Kent, Ohio: Kent State University Pr., 1970. (*Serif Series,* 12)

See also: Bryer, *Fifteen Modern American Authors* (A29), pp. 425-456.

WOOLF, VIRGINIA

B227   Beebe, Maurice. "Criticism of Virginia Woolf: A Selected Checklist with an Index to Studies of Separate Works," *Modern Fiction Studies,* II, No. 1 (1956), 36-45.

WORDSWORTH, WILLIAM

B228   Logan, James V[enable]. *Wordsworthian Criticism: A Guide and Bibliography.* Columbus: Ohio State University Pr., 1961, pp. 157-275. (*Graduate School Monographs. Contributions in Languages and Literature,* 12)

B229   Henley, Elton F. and David H. Stam. *Wordsworthian Criticism, 1945-1964: An Annotated Bibliography.* Rev. ed. N.Y.: New York Public Library, 1965.

See also: Raysor, *The English Romantic Poets* (A69), pp. 38-74.

YEATS, WILLIAM BUTLER

B230   Gerstenberger, Donna. "Yeats and the Theater: A Selected Bibliography." *Modern Drama,* VI, No. 1-4 (1963), 64-71.

B231   Cross, K. G. W. "The Fascination of What's Difficult: A Survey of Yeats Criticism and Research," in A[lexander] Norman Jeffers and K. G. W. Cross, eds. *In Excited Reverie: A Centenary Tribute to William Butler Yeats, 1865-1939.* N.Y.: Macmillan, 1965, pp. 315-337.

B232   Stallworthy, Jon. "A Short Guide to Yeats Studies", *The Critical Survey,* III, No. 1 (1966), 17-22.

FURTHER REFERENCES ON AUTHORS

In addition to bibliographies and checklists, there are also many handbooks, glossaries, and dictionaries on individual authors. Many contain selected bibliographies, and often include biographical information, summaries of sources and analogues, plot summaries, identification of personal names and place names, and the meanings of foreign words, allusions, and puns. Some of the best known are James Holly Hanford's *A Milton Handbook*, Robert D. French's *A Chaucer Handbook*, and F. E. Halliday's *A Shakespeare Companion*. There are also many collections of articles on individual authors in various publishers' series. These are often convenient to use, but uneven in quality. They fall into the following categories:

I CASEBOOKS

The casebook is usually concerned with one specific work or the selected poetry of one author and supplies primary documents, a selection of articles, and suggestions for further reading. There are several publishers' series, notably the "Crowell Literary Casebooks," "Harbrace Sourcebooks," and the "Norton Critical Editions." Scott, Foresman and Co., and the Odyssey Pr. have also published several excellent casebooks.

II READER'S GUIDES

Each guide is a detailed series of studies by one scholar on the works of a particular author. The American publisher is Noonday Pr., a division of Farrar, Straus and Giroux; the British publisher is Thames and Hudson.

The "Twayne's Authors Series," including American, English, and European authors, is similar in type to the "Reader's Guides." This series sometimes contains good selective bibliographies providing both primary and secondary sources.

III COLLECTIONS

There are many collections of articles by several scholars on the works of one specific author, selected and edited by one person. Two outstanding series are: "Discussions of Literature" edited by Joseph H. Summers, and published by D. C. Heath and Co., and "Twentieth Century Views," edited by Maynard Mack, and published by Prentice-Hall.

GLOSSARY

Abstract

> A summary giving the essential points of a book, pamphlet, or article, in order that a researcher or specialist may have a clear idea of its potential value to him. An extension of *Annotation.*

Annotation

> A concise descriptive or critical note about a book, pamphlet, or article. A bibliography containing content descriptions or critical evaluations of the items cited is called an "annotated bibliography."

Bibliography

> The term is often used synonymously with *Checklist*, but a bibliography is considered to be more complete in physical description and in coverage. Though there are many kinds of bibliography (among them: trade, national, and analytical or descriptive), the student is most frequently concerned with "enumerative" bibliographies providing a list of materials about a subject, period or author and containing *Primary Sources* or *Secondary Sources* or both. It may or may not be annotated and it may be in the form of either a list or an essay. Evaluative surveys such as *YWES* are known as bibliographic essays.

Bio-Bibliography

> A biographical outline of an author (or many authors), containing a list of the author's works.

Casebook

> Concerned with one specific work or several poems by one author, it usually reprints definitive text, primary documents, reviews, controversial articles, often with a running commentary by the editor, a good bibliography of *Primary* and *Secondary Sources*, and a list of questions for consideration.

Checklist

> A list of books, periodicals, or other material, generally somewhat tentative, with the minimum of description and annotation needed for identification of the works recorded.

Concordance

An alphabetical verbal index showing the places in the text of a book where each principal word may be found often with its immediate context.

Cumulative Index

A merging of two or more indexes to form one alphabet, in order that the user will save the time spent in consulting several issues.

Definitive Edition

Detailed, scholarly edition, recognized as the final, authoritative text. An edition that records textual variants and contains critical introductions and explanatory notes.

Edition

A printed production the same as an earlier one in title but produced from a new type-setting with substantial changes or additions to the text. This term should not be confused with "reprint"—a subsequent printing from the same type-setting or plates, having the identical text as the previous printing.

Encyclopedic Dictionary

See *Handbook*

Festschrift

Volume of writings contributed by students, colleagues, and admirers to honour a scholar on a special anniversary.

Footnote

A note containing a reference to one or more works used as sources for a given subject, or locating quotations used within the text.

Genre

A distinctive type or category of literary composition—e.g., novel, poem, essay, short story, play.

Guide

An annotated list of bibliographies and other reference works instructing the student or researcher on the methods and materials of research.

Handbook

> A brief guide to "facts" on authors, plots, characters, allusions, literary terms, quotations, and so forth; less comprehensive than an encyclopedia. The terms "encyclopedia" and "dictionary" are sometimes used loosely with the meaning "handbook".

Monograph

> Usually denotes any separate bibliographic entity (book, pamphlet, or treatise) treating one subject or a single aspect of a subject. This term is often misused.

Periodical

> The American Library Association defines a periodical as "a *Serial* appearing or intended to appear indefinitely at regular or stated intervals, generally more frequently than annually, each issue of which normally contains separate articles, stories, or other writings."—*Anglo-American Cataloging Rules.*

> The terms "journal" and "magazine" are used synonymously with "periodical". Newspapers, or proceedings, transactions, and other papers of a corporate body, are not included in this term.

Primary Source

> An author's works, letters, memoirs, either published or in manuscript form. Any eye-witness account, such as newspaper editorials, government documents, broadsheets, pamphlets, etc., that reflect contemporary opinions on politics, religion, education, status of women, and so forth. Such sources can be invaluable to the literary researcher as well as to the historian.

Reprint

> See *Edition*

Secondary Source

> Books, articles, essays, theses, etc., about an author, a work, or theme. Evaluations and interpretations of *Primary Source* material.

Serial

> The American Library Association defines a serial as "a

publication issued in successive parts bearing numerical or chronological designations and intended to be continued indefinitely. Serials include *Periodicals*, newspapers, annuals (reports, yearbooks, etc.), the journals, memoirs, proceedings, transactions, etc, of societies, and numbered monographic series."—*Anglo-American Cataloging Rules.*

Standard Work

This may be the best available edition of an author, and may not necessarily be definitive, or it may be a basic work of lasting value on a special subject.

Symposium

A meeting or conference at which several speakers deliver short addresses on related topics or on various aspects of the same topic. Therefore "symposia" often refers to the published papers of such a conference.

Variorum Edition

An edition that gathers in condensed form explanatory and critical notes of various commentators and editors on difficult or doubtful passages. Among others, there are variorum editions for the works of Shakespeare and Spenser, and a variorum edition of Pope's *Dunciad.*

INDEXES

INDEX TO AUTHORS AS CONTRIBUTORS

This index lists authors, editors, compilers, and titles when used as a main entry. A few items often identified by either author or title are indexed by both. References are to item numbers rather than to page numbers.

INDEX TO AUTHORS AS SUBJECTS

This index to authors as subjects lists over 250 authors (including all authors within section B), and refers the student to citations in specialized, retrospective bibliographies only. The index excludes serial bibliographies covering more than one author. If an author is best known for one genre, citations to other genres are not indexed. For example, since the undergraduate would study Fielding as a novelist, we have excluded any references to sources citing him as a dramatist. Yeats is studied as a poet and a dramatist, and Hardy as a novelist and a poet; these authors are therefore indexed more fully. References are to item numbers, rather than page numbers. Italicized numbers refer to the section on individual authors (Section B).

James, Henry, A18, A31, A33, A101,
A102, A104, A108, A114-A116,
A238, A299, A301, *B105, B106*
Jeffers, Robinson, A31, A107, A115,
A299
Johnson, Samuel, A18, A65, A97,
A100, A114, A117, A224, A301,
A302, *B107, B108*
Jonson, Ben, A18, A57, A60, A83,
A89, A95, A107, A114, A117,
A220, A222, *B109-B111*
Joyce, James, A85, A100, A104,
A108, A116, A238, A265, A299,
B112-B116

Keats, John, A18, A67, A69, A107,
A114, A117, A224, A232, A302,
B117, B118
Kipling, Rudyard, A18, A72, A73,
A108, A114, A116, A238, A299,
B119
Klein, A. M., A38, A40, A42, A113
Kyd, Thomas, A18, A57, A58, A60,
A83, A85, A89, A95, A114, A117,
A222

Lamb, Charles, A18, A67, A68,
A114, A117, A224, A232, A301,
A302
Lampman, Archibald, A40, A42,
A113
Landor, Walter Savage, A18, A67,
A68, A107, A114, A117, A224,
A232
Langland, William, A18, A45, A48,
A49, A114, A117, A216, A217,
B120
Laurence, Margaret, A42
Lawrence, D. H., A100, A104, A108,
A116, A238, A265, A299,
B121-B123
Layton, Irving, A38, A40, A42
Leacock, Stephen, A40, A42, A113
Levertov, Denise, A115, A116, A126
Lewis, Cecil Day, A107, A116, A126
Lewis, Matthew Gregory (Monk),
A114, A224
Lewis, Sinclair, A31, A101, A103,
A115, *B124, B125*

Livesay, Dorothy, A40, A42, A113
Lodge, Thomas, A18, A57, A58,
A60, A83, A114, A117, A220,
A221, A222
Longfellow, Henry Wadsworth, A18,
A31, A107, A114, A117
Lovelace, Richard, A107, A114,
A117, A220, A222
Lowell, James Russell, A18, A31,
A107, A114
Lowell, Robert, A31, A107, A115,
A126
Lowry, Malcolm, A40, A42, A116,
B126
Lydgate, John, A18, A48, A49, A117
Lyly, John, A18, A57, A58, A60,
A95, A100, A114, A117, A221,
A222

Macaulay, Thomas Babbington, A18,
A72, A117
MacLeish, Archibald, A31, A107,
A115, A126, A299
MacLennan, Hugh, A40, A113, *B127*
MacNeice, Louis, A31, A107, A116,
A299
Malamud, Bernard, A103, A108,
A115, A126, *B128*
Malory, Sir Thomas, A18, A45, A48,
A49, A114, A117, A214, A215,
A217
Mansfield, Katherine, A108, A116,
A265, A299, *B129*
Marlowe, Christopher, A18, A57,
A58, A60, A83, A85, A89, A95,
A107, A114, A117, A221, A222,
B130
Marvell, Andrew, A18, A56, A57,
A59, A107, A114, A117, A220,
A222, A227, *B131, B132*
Maugham, Somerset, A100, A108,
A116, A126, *B133*
Melville, Herman, A31, A33, A101,
A102, A108, A117, *B134-B138*
Meredith, George, A18, A72, A74,
A76, A100, A108, A114, A117,
B139, B140
Middleton, Thomas, A18, A57, A60,
A83, A85, A89, A95, A114, A117,
A222

Mill, John Stuart, A18, A72, A114,
  A117, A302, *B141*
Millay, Edna St. Vincent, A31, A107,
  A115, A299, *B142*
Miller, Arthur, A31, A85, A87, A88,
  A90, A98, A115, A126, A282,
  B143, B144
Miller, Henry, A31, A101, A103,
  A115, A126, *B145*
Milton, John, A18, A85, A97, A107,
  A114, A117, A220, A222, A276,
  B146-B150
Mitchell, W. O., A42, A113
Moodie, Susannah, A40, A42
Moore, Brian, A42, A113, A126
Moore, George, A76, A83, A100,
  A114, A116, A299, *B151*
Moore, Marianne, A107, A115,
  A126, *B152*
Moore, Thomas, A67, A68
More, Sir Thomas, A18, A58, A117,
  A221, A222
Morris, William, A18, A72, A73,
  A74, A75, A107, A114, A117,
  B153
Mowat, Farley, A42, A113
Murdoch, Iris, A116, A126, A265,
  B154, B155

Nabokov, Vladimir, A103, A115,
  A126, *B156*
Nashe, Thomas, A18, A57, A58,
  A60, A107, A117, A221, A222
Newman, John Henry, A18, A72,
  A107, A114, A117
Nin, Anais, A115, A126

O'Casey, Sean, A83, A85, A89, A91,
  A98, A116, *B157*
O'Connor, Flannery, A32, A101,
  A103, A108, A115, A126
Odets, Clifford, A31, A85, A87, A88,
  A90, A98, A115
O'Neill, Eugene, A29, A31, A83,
  A85, A87, A88, A90, A98, A115,
  B158-B160
Orwell, George, A100, A108, A265,
  B161
Osborne, John, A98, A116, A126

Paine, Thomas, A18, A31, A114,
  A117
Pater, Walter Horatio, A18, A72,
  A108, A114, A117
Peacock, Thomas Love, A18, A100,
  A117, A224, A232
Pearl Poet, A45, A48, A215, A216,
  A217
Peele, George, A18, A57, A60, A95,
  A114, A117, A221, A222
Pepys, Samuel, A18, A114, A117,
  A222, A227
Pickthall, Marjorie, A40, A113
Pinter, Harold, A85, A89, A91, A98,
  A116, A126, *B162*
Poe, Edgar Allan, A18, A31, A32,
  A33, A102, A107, A108, A114,
  A117, A276, A302, *B163, B164*
Pope, Alexander, A18, A65, A107,
  A114, A117, A223, A224, A301,
  B165
Porter, Katherine Anne, A31, A32,
  A103, A104, A108, A115, A126,
  B166
Pound, Ezra, A29, A31, A107, A115,
  A126, A299, *B167*
Pratt, E. J., A40, A42, A113

Radcliffe, Mrs. Ann, A18, A65,
  A100, A117, A224
Reaney, James, A42, A85, A113
Rice, Elmer, A31, A85, A87, A88,
  A90, A98, A115
Richardson, Samuel, A18, A63, A65,
  A97, A100, A114, A224, A276
Richler, Mordecai, A38, A40, A42,
  A113
Roberts, Charles G. D., A40, A113
Robinson, Edwin Arlington, A29,
  A131, A107, A115, A299, *B168*
Ross, Sinclair, A40, A113
Rossetti, Christina, A18, A72-A75,
  A107, A114, A117
Rossetti, Dante Gabriel, A18, A72-
  A75, A107, A114, A117
Roy, Gabrielle, A40, A42
Ruskin, John, A18, A72, A75, A114,
  A117, A302